DOVER · THRIFT · EDITIONS

Great Love Poems

Edited by Shane Weller

DOVER PUBLICATIONS, INC.
New York

Note

The present anthology offers a selection of short poems written in English between the Renaissance and the present day on the subject of carnal love, or the desire of one human being for another. The poems fall into two broad categories: those reflecting on the nature of love and those written from the standpoint (whether real or imaginary) of the lover. The selection seeks to represent the high points in the tradition of love poetry and to give a sense of the great diversity within that tradition. The poems are arranged chronologically by poet.

DOVER THRIFT EDITIONS

GENERAL EDITOR: STANLEY APPELBAUM

Acknowledgments

"Carrier Letter" is reprinted from *The Complete Poems and Selected Letters and Prose of Hart Crane*, edited by Brom Weber, by permission of Liveright Publishing Corporation. Copyright 1933, © 1958, 1966 by Liveright Publishing Corporation.

" 'I, Being Born a Woman and Distressed' " by Edna St. Vincent Millay is reprinted from *Collected Poems*, Harper & Row. Copyright 1923, 1951 by Edna St. Vincent Millay and Norma Millay Ellis. Reprinted by permission of Elizabeth Barnett, literary executor.

"Piazza Piece" is reprinted from *Selected Poems* by John Crowe Ransom. Copyright 1927 by Alfred A. Knopf, Inc., and renewed 1955 by John Crowe Ransom. Reprinted by permission of Alfred A. Knopf, Inc., and Carcanet Press Limited, United Kingdom.

Published in Canada by General Publishing Company, Ltd., 30 Lesmill Road, Don Mills, Toronto, Ontario.
Published in the United Kingdom by Constable and Company, Ltd., 3 The Lanchesters, 162–164 Fulham Palace Road, London W6 9ER.

This new anthology, first published by Dover Publications, Inc., in 1992, contains 161 poems reprinted (with the exception of those poems listed in the Acknowledgments above) from standard editions.

Manufactured in the United States of America
Dover Publications, Inc., 31 East 2nd Street, Mineola, N.Y. 11501

Library of Congress Cataloging-in-Publication Data

Great love poems / edited by Shane Weller.
    p.   cm. — (Dover thrift editions)
  Includes index.
  ISBN 0-486-27284-2 (pbk.)
  1. Love poetry, English. I. Weller, Shane. II. Series.
PR1184.G68   1992
821.008′0354—dc20
                                                  92-31455
                                                  CIP

Contents

iii

SIR THOMAS WYATT
(1503–1542)

The Lover Showeth How He Is Forsaken of Such as He Sometime Enjoyed

They flee from me that sometime did me seek,
   With naked foot stalking in my chamber.
I have seen them gentle, tame, and meek,
   That now are wild, and do not once remember
   That sometime they have put themselves in danger
To take bread at my hand; and now they range,
Busily seeking with a continual change.

Thanked be fortune, it hath been otherwise
   Twenty times better; but once, in special,
In thin array, after a pleasant guise,
   When her loose gown from her shoulders did fall,
   And she me caught in her arms long and small,
Therewith all sweetly did me kiss,
And softly said, 'Dear heart, how like you this?'

It was no dream; I lay broad waking:
   But all is turned, thorough my gentleness,
Into a strange fashion of forsaking;
   And I have leave to go, of her goodness;
   And she also to use new-fangleness.
But since that I so unkindly am served,
I fain would know what she hath deserved.

The Appeal

An Earnest Suit to His Unkind Mistress,
Not to Forsake Him

And wilt thou leave me thus?
Say nay, say nay, for shame!
—To save thee from the blame
Of all my grief and grame. [1]
And wilt thou leave me thus?
   Say nay! say nay!

And wilt thou leave me thus,
That hath loved thee so long
In wealth and woe among?
And is thy heart so strong
As for to leave me thus?
   Say nay! say nay!

And wilt thou leave me thus,
That hath given thee my heart
Never for to depart
Neither for pain nor smart:
And wilt thou leave me thus?
   Say nay! say nay!

And wilt thou leave me thus,
And have no more pity
Of him that loveth thee?
Alas, thy cruelty!
And wilt thou leave me thus?
   Say nay! say nay!

[1] *grame*] sorrow.

EDMUND SPENSER
(1552–1599)

'One Day I Wrote Her Name upon the Strand'

One day I wrote her name upon the strand,
    But came the waves and washed it away:
Again I wrote it with a second hand,
    But came the tide, and made my pains his prey.
'Vain man,' said she, 'that dost in vain assay
    A mortal thing so to immortalize,
For I myself shall like to this decay,
    And eke my name be wiped out likewise.'
'Not so,' quod I, 'let baser things devise
    To die in dust, but you shall live by fame:
My verse your virtues rare shall eternize,
    And in the heavens write your glorious name;
Where, whenas Death shall all the world subdue,
    Our love shall live, and later life renew.'

SIR WALTER RALEIGH
(1552?–1618)

" 'As Ye Came from the Holy Land' "

    'As ye came from the holy land
        Of Walsinghame,
    Met you not with my true love
        By the way as you came?'

    'How should I know your true love,
        That have met many a one
    As I came from the holy land,
        That have come, that have gone?'

'She is neither white nor brown,
    But as the heavens fair;
There is none hath her form divine
    In the earth or the air.'

'Such a one did I meet, good sir,
    Such an angelic face,
Who like a nymph, like a queen, did appear
    In her gait, in her grace.'

'She hath left me here alone,
    All alone, as unknown,
Who sometime did me lead with herself,
    And me loved as her own.'

'What's the cause that she leaves you alone
    And a new way doth take,
That sometime did love you as her own,
    And her joy did you make?'

'I have loved her all my youth,
    But now am old, as you see:
Love likes not the falling fruit,
    Nor the withered tree.

'Know that Love is a careless child,
    And forgets promise past;
He is blind, he is deaf when he list,
    And in faith never fast.

'His desire is a dureless content,
    And a trustless joy;
He is won with a world of despair,
    And is lost with a toy.

'Of womenkind such indeed is the love,
    Or the word love abused,
Under which many childish desires
    And conceits are excused.

'But true love is a durable fire,
    In the mind ever burning,
Never sick, never dead, never cold,
    From itself never turning.'

Her Reply[1]

If all the world and love were young,
And truth in every shepherd's tongue,
These pretty pleasures might me move
To live with thee and be thy Love.

But Time drives flocks from field to fold;
When rivers rage and rocks grow cold;
And Philomel becometh dumb;
The rest complains of cares to come.

The flowers do fade, and wanton fields
To wayward Winter reckoning yields:
A honey tongue, a heart of gall,
Is fancy's spring, but sorrow's fall.

Thy gowns, thy shoes, thy beds of roses,
Thy cap, thy kirtle, and thy posies,
Soon break, soon wither—soon forgotten,
In folly ripe, in reason rotten.

Thy belt of straw and ivy-buds,
Thy coral clasps and amber studs,—
All these in me no means can move
To come to thee and be thy Love.

But could youth last, and love still breed,
Had joys no date, nor age no need,
Then these delights my mind might move
To live with thee and be thy Love.

[1] This poem is a response to Marlowe's "The Passionate Shepherd to His Love" (see page 10).

SIR PHILIP SIDNEY
(1554–1586)

'Loving in Truth, and Fain in Verse My Love to Show'

Loving in truth, and fain in verse my love to show,
That the dear she might take some pleasure of my pain,
Pleasure might cause her read, reading might make her know,
Knowledge might pity win, and pity grace obtain,
I sought fit words to paint the blackest face of woe:
Studying inventions fine, her wits to entertain,
Oft turning others' leaves, to see if thence would flow
Some fresh and fruitful showers upon my sunburned brain.
But words came halting forth, wanting Invention's stay;
Invention, Nature's child, fled stepdame Study's blows;
And others' feet still seemed but strangers in my way.
Thus, great with child to speak, and helpless in my throes,
　　Biting my truant pen, beating myself for spite:
　　'Fool,' said my Muse to me, 'look in thy heart, and write.'

His Lady's Cruelty

With how sad steps, O Moon, thou climb'st the skies!
How silently, and with how wan a face!
What! may it be that even in heavenly place
That busy archer his sharp arrows tries?
Sure, if that long-with-love-acquainted eyes
Can judge of love, thou feel'st a lover's case:
I read it in thy looks; thy languish'd grace
To me, that feel the like, thy state descries.
Then, even of fellowship, O Moon, tell me,
Is constant love deem'd there but want of wit?
Are beauties there as proud as here they be?
Do they above love to be loved, and yet
　　Those lovers scorn whom that love doth possess?
　　Do they call 'virtue' there—ungratefulness?

The Bargain

My true love hath my heart, and I have his,
    By just exchange one for another given;
I hold his dear, and mine he cannot miss,
    There never was a better bargain driven:
        My true love hath my heart, and I have his.

His heart in me keeps him and me in one,
    My heart in him his thoughts and senses guides;
He loves my heart, for once it was his own,
    I cherish his because in me it bides:
        My true love hath my heart, and I have his.

JOHN LYLY
(1554?–1606)

Cards and Kisses

Cupid and my Campaspe play'd
At cards for kisses—Cupid paid:
He stakes his quiver, bow, and arrows,
His mother's doves, and team of sparrows;
Loses them too; then down he throws
The coral of his lips, the rose
Growing on's cheek (but none knows how);
With these, the crystal of his brow,
And then the dimple of his chin:
All these did my Campaspe win.
At last he set her both his eyes—
She won, and Cupid blind did rise.
    O Love! has she done this for thee?
    What shall, alas! become of me?

GEORGE PEELE
(1556–1596)

A Summer Song

When as the rye reach to the chin,
And chopcherry, chopcherry ripe within,
Strawberries swimming in the cream,
And school-boys playing in the stream;
Then O, then O, then O my true love said,
Till that time come again,
She could not live a maid.

HENRY CONSTABLE
(1562–1613)

Diaphenia

Diaphenia like the daffadowndilly,
  White as the sun, fair as the lily,
Heigh ho, how I do love thee!
  I do love thee as my lambs
  Are beloved of their dams;
How blest were I if thou wouldst prove me.

Diaphenia like the spreading roses,
  That in thy sweets all sweets encloses,
Fair sweet, how I do love thee!
  I do love thee as each flower
  Loves the sun's life-giving power;
For dead, thy breath to life might move me.

Diaphenia like to all things blessed
  When all thy praises are expressed,
Dear joy, how I do love thee!
  As the birds do love the spring,
  Or the bees their careful king:
Then in requite, sweet virgin, love me!

SAMUEL DANIEL
(1562?–1619)

'If This Be Love, to Draw a Weary Breath'

If this be love, to draw a weary breath,
To paint on floods till the shore cry to th'air,
With downward looks, still reading on the earth
The sad memorials of my love's despair;
If this be love, to war against my soul,
Lie down to wail, rise up to sigh and grieve,
The never-resting stone of care to roll,
Still to complain my griefs whilst none relieve;
If this be love, to clothe me with dark thoughts,
Haunting untrodden paths to wail apart;
My pleasures horror, music tragic notes,
Tears in mine eyes and sorrow at my heart.
    If this be love, to live a living death,
    Then do I love and draw this weary breath.

MICHAEL DRAYTON
(1563–1631)

The Parting

Since there's no help, come let us kiss and part—
Nay, I have done, you get no more of me;
And I am glad, yea, glad with all my heart,
That thus so cleanly I myself can free.
Shake hands for ever, cancel all our vows,
And when we meet at any time again,
Be it not seen in either of our brows
That we one jot of former love retain.
Now at the last gasp of Love's latest breath,
When, his pulse failing, Passion speechless lies,
When Faith is kneeling by his bed of death,

And Innocence is closing up his eyes,
   —Now if thou wouldst, when all have given him over,
From death to life thou might'st him yet recover.

CHRISTOPHER MARLOWE
(1564–1593)

The Passionate Shepherd to His Love

Come live with me and be my Love,
And we will all the pleasures prove
That hills and valleys, dales and fields,
Or woods or steepy mountain yields.

And we will sit upon the rocks,
And see the shepherds feed their flocks
By shallow rivers, to whose falls
Melodious birds sing madrigals.

And I will make thee beds of roses
And a thousand fragrant posies;
A cap of flowers, and a kirtle
Embroider'd all with leaves of myrtle.

A gown made of the finest wool
Which from our pretty lambs we pull;
Fair-lined slippers for the cold,
With buckles of the purest gold.

A belt of straw and ivy-buds
With coral clasps and amber studs:
And if these pleasures may thee move,
Come live with me and be my Love.

The shepherd swains shall dance and sing
For thy delight each May morning:
If these delights thy mind may move,
Then live with me and be my Love.

WILLIAM SHAKESPEARE
(1564–1616)

'Shall I Compare Thee to a Summer's Day?'

Shall I compare thee to a summer's day?
Thou art more lovely and more temperate:
Rough winds do shake the darling buds of May,
And summer's lease hath all too short a date:
Sometime too hot the eye of heaven shines,
And often is his gold complexion dimm'd;
And every fair from fair sometime declines,
By chance, or nature's changing course, untrimm'd;
But thy eternal summer shall not fade,
Nor lose possession of that fair thou owest;
Nor shall Death brag thou wander'st in his shade,
When in eternal lines to time thou growest;
    So long as men can breathe, or eyes can see,
    So long lives this, and this gives life to thee.

'That Time of Year Thou Mayst in Me Behold'

That time of year thou mayst in me behold
When yellow leaves, or none, or few, do hang
Upon those boughs which shake against the cold,
Bare ruin'd choirs, where late the sweet birds sang.
In me thou seest the twilight of such day
As after sunset fadeth in the west,
Which by and by black night doth take away,
Death's second self, that seals up all in rest.
In me thou seest the glowing of such fire,
That on the ashes of his youth doth lie,
As the death-bed whereon it must expire,
Consum'd with that which it was nourish'd by.
    This thou perceiv'st which makes thy love more strong,
    To love that well which thou must leave ere long.

'From You Have I Been Absent in the Spring'

From you have I been absent in the spring,
When proud-pied April, dress'd in all his trim,
Hath put a spirit of youth in everything,
That heavy Saturn laugh'd and leap'd with him.
Yet nor the lays of birds, nor the sweet smell
Of different flowers in odour and in hue,
Could make me any summer's story tell,
Or from their proud lap pluck them where they grew:
Nor did I wonder at the lilies white,
Nor praise the deep vermilion in the rose;
They were but sweet, but figures of delight,
Drawn after you, you pattern of all those.
     Yet seem'd it winter still, and you, away,
     As with your shadow I with these did play.

'When in the Chronicle of Wasted Time'

When in the chronicle of wasted time
I see descriptions of the fairest wights,
And beauty making beautiful old rhyme,
In praise of ladies dead and lovely knights,
Then in the blazon of sweet beauty's best,
Of hand, of foot, of lip, of eye, of brow,
I see their antique pen would have express'd
Even such a beauty as you master now.
So all their praises are but prophecies
Of this our time, all you prefiguring;
And, for they look'd but with divining eyes,
They had not skill enough your worth to sing:
     For we, which now behold these present days,
     Have eyes to wonder, but lack tongues to praise.

'Let Me Not to the Marriage of True Minds'

Let me not to the marriage of true minds
Admit impediments. Love is not love
Which alters when it alteration finds,
Or bends with the remover to remove:
O no; it is an ever-fixed mark,
That looks on tempests, and is never shaken;
It is the star to every wandering bark,
Whose worth's unknown, although his height be taken,
Love's not Time's fool, though rosy lips and cheeks
Within his bending sickle's compass come;
Love alters not with his brief hours and weeks,
But bears it out even to the edge of doom.
　　If this be error, and upon me prov'd,
　　I never writ, nor no man ever lov'd.

'My Mistress' Eyes Are Nothing Like the Sun'

My mistress' eyes are nothing like the sun;
Coral is far more red than her lips' red:
If snow be white, why then her breasts are dun;
If hairs be wires, black wires grow on her head.
I have seen roses damask'd, red and white,
But no such roses see I in her cheeks;
And in some perfumes is there more delight
Than in the breath that from my mistress reeks.
I love to hear her speak,—yet well I know
That music hath a far more pleasing sound;
I grant I never saw a goddess go,—
My mistress when she walks, treads on the ground;
　　And yet, by heaven, I think my love as rare
　　As any she belied with false compare.

THOMAS CAMPION
(1567–1620)

Cherry-Ripe

There is a garden in her face
   Where roses and white lilies blow;
A heavenly paradise is that place,
   Wherein all pleasant fruits do flow;
     There cherries grow which none may buy
     Till 'Cherry-ripe' themselves do cry.

Those cherries fairly do enclose
   Of orient pearls a double row,
Which when her lovely laughter shows,
   They look like rose-buds fill'd with snow;
     Yet them nor peer nor prince can buy
     Till 'Cherry-ripe' themselves do cry.

Her eyes like angels watch them still;
   Her brows like bended bows do stand,
Threat'ning with piercing frowns to kill
   All that attempt with eye or hand
     Those sacred cherries to come nigh,
     Till 'Cherry-ripe' themselves do cry.

'Thou Art Not Fair, for All Thy Red and White'

Thou art not fair, for all thy red and white,
For all those rosy ornaments in thee;
Thou art not sweet, though made of mere delight,
Not fair nor sweet, unless thou pity me.
I will not soothe thy fancies: thou shalt prove
That beauty is no beauty without love.

Yet love not me, nor seek thou to allure
My thoughts with beauty, were it more divine:

Thy smiles and kisses I cannot endure,
I'll not be wrapt up in those arms of thine:
Now show it, if thou be a woman right,—
Embrace, and kiss, and love me, in despite!

Vobiscum est Iope

When thou must home to shades of underground,
And there arrived, a new admired guest,
The beauteous spirits do engirt thee round,
White Iope, blithe Helen, and the rest,
To hear the stories of thy finish'd love
From that smooth tongue whose music hell can move;

Then wilt thou speak of banqueting delights,
Of masques and revels which sweet youth did make,
Of tourneys and great challenges of knights,
And all these triumphs for thy beauty's sake:
When thou hast told these honours done to thee,
Then tell, O tell, how thou didst murder me!

SIR HENRY WOTTON
(1568–1639)

Elizabeth of Bohemia

You meaner beauties of the night,
   That poorly satisfy our eyes
More by your number than your light,
   You common people of the skies;
     What are you when the moon shall rise?

You curious chanters of the wood,
   That warble forth Dame Nature's lays,
Thinking your passions understood
   By your weak accents; what's your praise
     When Philomel her voice shall raise?

You violets that first appear,
  By your pure purple mantles known
Like the proud virgins of the year,
  As if the spring were all your own;
  What are you when the rose is blown?

So, when my mistress shall be seen
  In form and beauty of her mind,
By virtue first, then choice, a Queen,
  Tell me, if she were not design'd
  Th'eclipse and glory of her kind?

JOHN DONNE
(1572–1631)

The Sun Rising

Busy old fool, unruly Sun,
  Why dost thou thus,
Through windows, and through curtains call on us?
Must to thy motions lovers' seasons run?
  Saucy pedantic wretch, go chide
  Late school-boys, and sour 'prentices,
 Go tell court-huntsmen that the King will ride,
 Call country ants to harvest offices;
Love, all alike, no season knows, nor clime,
Nor hours, days, months, which are the rags of time.

Thy beams, so reverend, and strong
  Why shouldst thou think?
I could eclipse and cloud them with a wink,
But that I would not lose her sight so long:
  If her eyes have not blinded thine,
  Look, and tomorrow late, tell me,
 Whether both the Indias of spice and mine
 Be where thou left'st them, or lie here with me.
Ask for those kings whom thou saw'st yesterday,
And thou shalt hear, 'All here in one bed lay.'

She is all States, and all Princes, I;
　　Nothing else is.
Princes do but play us; compar'd to this,
All honour's mimic; all wealth alchemy.
　　Thou Sun art half as happy as we,
　　In that the world's contracted thus;
　Thine age asks ease, and since thy duties be
　To warm the world, that's done in warming us.
Shine here to us, and thou art every where;
This bed thy centre is, these walls, thy sphere.

The Canonization

For Godsake hold your tongue, and let me love,
　　Or chide my palsy, or my gout,
My five gray hairs, or ruin'd fortune flout,
　　With wealth your state, your mind with arts improve,
　　　Take you a course, get you a place,
　　　Observe his honour, or his grace,
　Or the King's real, or his stamped face
　　Contemplate, what you will, approve,
　　So you will let me love.

Alas, alas, who's injur'd by my love?
　　What merchants' ships have my sighs drown'd?
Who says my tears have overflow'd his ground?
　　When did my colds a forward spring remove?
　　　When did the heats which my veins fill
　　　Add one more to the plaguey bill?
Soldiers find wars, and lawyers find out still
　　Litigious men, which quarrels move,
　　Though she and I do love.

Call us what you will, we are made such by love;
　　Call her one, me another fly,
We are tapers too, and at our own cost die,
　　And we in us find the eagle and the dove.
　　　The phoenix riddle hath more wit
　　　By us, we two being one, are it.

So to one neutral thing both sexes fit,
   We die and rise the same, and prove
   Mysterious by this love.

We can die by it, if not live by love,
   And if unfit for tombs and hearse
Our legend be, it will be fit for verse;
   And if no piece of chronicle we prove,
     We'll build in sonnets pretty rooms;
     As well a well wrought urn becomes
The greatest ashes, as half-acre tombs,
   And by these hymns, all shall approve
   Us *canoniz'd* for love:

And thus invoke us; You whom reverend love
   Made one another's hermitage;
You, to whom love was peace, that now is rage;
   Who did the whole world's soul contract, and drove
     Into the glasses of your eyes
     (So made such mirrors, and such spies,
That they did all to you epitomize,)
   Countries, towns, courts: Beg from above
   A pattern of your love!

Song

Sweetest love, I do not go
   For weariness of thee,
Nor in hope the world can show
   A fitter love for me;
     But since that I
Must die at last, 'tis best
To use myself in jest
   Thus by fained deaths to die.

Yesternight the sun went hence,
   And yet is here today,
He hath no desire nor sense,
   Nor half so short a way:
     Then fear not me,

But believe that I shall make
Speedier journeys, since I take
    More wings and spurs than he.

O how feeble is man's power,
    That if good fortune fall,
Cannot add another hour,
    Nor a lost hour recall!
        But come bad chance,
And we join to it our strength,
And we teach it art and length,
    Itself o'er us to advance.

When thou sigh'st, thou sigh'st not wind,
    But sigh'st my soul away,
When thou weep'st, unkindly kind,
    My life's blood doth decay.
        It cannot be
That thou lov'st me, as thou say'st,
If in thine my life thou waste,
    Thou art the best of me.

Let not thy divining heart
    Forethink me any ill,
Destiny may take thy part,
    And may thy fears fulfil;
        But think that we
Are but turned aside to sleep;
They who one another keep
    Alive, ne'er parted be.

The Apparition

When by thy scorn, O murd'ress, I am dead,
And that thou thinkst thee free
From all solicitation from me,
Then shall my ghost come to thy bed,
And thee, fain'd vestal, in worse arms shall see;
Then thy sick taper will begin to wink,

And he, whose thou art then, being tired before,
Will, if thou stir, or pinch to wake him, think
      Thou call'st for more,
And in false sleep will from thee shrink,
And then poor aspen wretch, neglected thou
Bath'd in a cold quicksilver sweat wilt lie
      A verier ghost than I;
What I will say I will not tell thee now,
Lest that preserve thee; and since my love is spent,
I had rather thou shouldst painfully repent,
Than by my threat'nings rest still innocent.

The Ecstasy

Where, like a pillow on a bed,
   A pregnant bank swell'd up, to rest
The violet's reclining head,
   Sat we two, one another's best.
Our hands were firmly cemented
   By a fast balm which thence did spring;
Our eye-beams twisted, and did thread
   Our eyes upon one double string.
So to engraft our hands, as yet
   Was all the means to make us one;
And pictures in our eyes to get
   Was all our propagation.
As 'twixt two equal armies Fate
   Suspends uncertain victory,
Our souls—which to advance their state
   Were gone out—hung 'twixt her and me.
And whilst our souls negotiate there,
   We like sepulchral statues lay;
All day the same our postures were,
   And we said nothing, all the day.
If any, so by love refined,
   That he soul's language understood,
And by good love were grown all mind,
   Within convenient distance stood,

He (though he knew not which soul spake,
   Because both meant, both spake the same)
Might thence a new concoction take,
   And part far purer than he came.
This Ecstasy doth unperplex
   (We said) and tell us what we love,
We see by this, it was not sex,
   We see, we saw not what did move:
But as all several souls contain
   Mixture of things, they know not what,
Love, these mixed souls doth mix again,
   And makes both one, each this and that.
A single violet transplant,
   The strength, the colour, and the size
(All which before was poor and scant)
   Redoubles still, and multiplies.
When love, with one another so
   Interinanimates two souls,
That abler soul, which thence doth flow,
   Defects of loneliness controls.
We then, who are this new soul, know,
   Of what we are composed and made,
For th'Atomies of which we grow,
   Are souls, whom no change can invade.
But O alas, so long, so far
   Our bodies why do we forbear?
They are ours, though they are not we; we are
   The intelligences, they the sphere.
We owe them thanks, because they thus,
   Did us, to us, at first convey,
Yielded their forces, sense, to us,
   Nor are dross to us, but allay.
On man heaven's influence works not so,
   But that it first imprints the air,
So soul into the soul may flow,
   Though it to body first repair.
As our blood labours to beget
   Spirits, as like souls as it can,
Because such fingers need to knit
   That subtle knot, which makes us man:
So must pure lovers' souls descend

T'affections, and to faculties,
    Which sense may reach and apprehend,
        Else a great Prince in prison lies.
To our bodies turn we then, that so
    Weak men on love revealed may look;
Love's mysteries in souls do grow,
    But yet the body is his book.
And if some lover, such as we,
    Have heard this dialogue of one,
Let him still mark us, he shall see
    Small change, when we are to bodies gone.

The Funeral

Whoever comes to shroud me, do not harm
        Nor question much
That subtle wreath of hair about mine arm;
The mystery, the sign you must not touch,
        For 'tis my outward soul,
Viceroy to that which, unto heav'n being gone,
        Will leave this to control
And keep these limbs, her provinces, from dissolution.

For if the sinewy thread my brain lets fall
        Through every part
Can tie those parts, and make me one of all,
Those hairs, which upward grew, and strength and art
        Have from a better brain,
Can better do't: except she meant that I
        By this should know my pain,
As prisoners then are manacled, when they're condemn'd to die.

Whate'er she meant by 't, bury it with me,
        For since I am
Love's martyr, it might breed idolatry
If into other hands these relics came.
        As 'twas humility
T'afford to it all that a soul can do,
        So 'tis some bravery
That, since you would have none of me, I bury some of you.

Elegy: On His Mistress Going to Bed

Come, Madam, come, all rest my powers defy,
Until I labour, I in labour lie.
The foe oft-times having the foe in sight
Is tired with standing though he never fight.
Off with that girdle, like heaven's zone glittering,
But a far fairer world incompassing.
Unpin that spangled breastplate which you wear,
That th'eyes of busy fools may be stopped there.
Unlace yourself, for that harmonious chime
Tells me from you that now it is bed time.
Off with that happy busk, which I envy,
That still can be, and still can stand so nigh.
Your gown going off such beauteous state reveals
As when from flow'ry meads th'hill's shadow steals.
Off with that wiry coronet and show
The hairy diadem which on you doth grow:
Now off with those shoes, and then safely tread
In this love's hallow'd temple, this soft bed.
In such white robes, heaven's angels us'd to be
Receiv'd by men; thou angel bring'st with thee
A heaven like Mahomet's paradise; and though
Ill spirits walk in white, we easily know
By this these angels from an evil sprite,
Those set our hairs, but these our flesh upright.
    License my roving hands, and let them go,
Before, behind, between, above, below.
O my America! my new-found-land,
My kingdom, safeliest when with one man mann'd,
My mine of precious stones, my empery,
How blest am I in this discovering thee!
To enter in these bonds, is to be free;
Then where my hand is set, my seal shall be.
    Full nakedness! All joys are due to thee,
As souls unbodied, bodies uncloth'd must be,
To taste whole joys. Gems which you women use
Are like Atlanta's balls, cast in men's views,
That when a fool's eye lighteth on a gem,

His earthly soul may covet theirs, not them.
Like pictures, or like books' gay coverings made
For lay-men, are all women thus array'd;
Themselves are mystic books, which only we
(Whom their imputed grace will dignify)
Must see reveal'd. Then since that I may know,
As liberally, as to a midwife, show
Thy self: cast all, yea, this white linen hence,
There is no penance due to innocence.
　　To teach thee, I am naked first; why then
What need'st thou have more covering than a man?

BEN JONSON
(1573?–1637)

To Celia

Drink to me only with thine eyes,
　　And I will pledge with mine;
Or leave a kiss but in the cup
　　And I'll not look for wine.
The thirst that from the soul doth rise
　　Doth ask a drink divine;
But might I of Jove's nectar sup,
　　I would not change for thine.

I sent thee late a rosy wreath,
　　Not so much honouring thee
As giving it a hope that there
　　It could not wither'd be;
But thou thereon didst only breathe,
　　And sent'st it back to me;
Since when it grows, and smells, I swear,
　　Not of itself but thee!

The Hour Glass

Consider this small dust, here in the glass,
    By atoms mov'd:
Could you believe that this the body was
    Of one that lov'd;
And in his mistress' flame playing like a fly,
Was turned to cinders by her eye:
Yes; and in death, as life unblest,
    To have 't exprest,
Even ashes of lovers find no rest.

THOMAS HEYWOOD
(1574?–1641)

Matin Song

Pack, clouds, away! and welcome, day!
    With night we banish sorrow.
Sweet air, blow soft; mount, lark, aloft
    To give my Love good-morrow!
Wings from the wind to please her mind,
    Notes from the lark I'll borrow;
Bird, prune thy wing! nightingale, sing!
    To give my Love good-morrow!
        To give my Love good-morrow
        Notes from them all I'll borrow.

Wake from thy nest, robin red-breast!
    Sing, birds, in every furrow!
And from each bill let music shrill
    Give my fair Love good-morrow!
Blackbird and thrush in every bush,
    Stare,[1] linnet, and cocksparrow,

---

[1] *Stare*] starling.

You pretty elves, among yourselves
   Sing my fair Love good-morrow!
      To give my Love good-morrow!
      Sing, birds, in every furrow!

GEORGE WITHER
(1588–1667)

'I Loved a Lass, a Fair One'

I loved a lass, a fair one,
   As fair as e'er was seen;
She was indeed a rare one,
   Another Sheba Queen:
But, fool as then I was,
   I thought she loved me too:
But now, alas! she's left me,
   Falero, lero, loo!

Her hair like gold did glister,
   Each eye was like a star,
She did surpass her sister,
   Which pass'd all others far;
She would me honey call,
   She'd—O she'd kiss me too!
But now, alas! she's left me,
   Falero, lero, loo!

Many a merry meeting
   My love and I have had;
She was my only sweeting,
   She made my heart full glad;
The tears stood in her eyes
   Like to the morning dew:
But now, alas! she's left me,
   Falero, lero, loo!

Her cheeks were like the cherry,
   Her skin was white as snow;

When she was blithe and merry
   She angel-like did show;
Her waist exceeding small,
   The fives did fit her shoe:
But now, alas! she's left me,
   Falero, lero, loo!

In summer time or winter
   She had her heart's desire;
I still did scorn to stint her
   From sugar, sack, or fire;
The world went round about,
   No cares we ever knew:
But now, alas! she's left me,
   Falero, lero, loo!

To maidens' vows and swearing
   Henceforth no credit give;
You may give them the hearing
   But never them believe;
They are as false as fair,
   Unconstant, frail, untrue:
For mine, alas! hath left me,
   Falero, lero, loo!

ROBERT HERRICK
(1591–1674)

To the Virgins, to Make Much of Time

Gather ye rosebuds while ye may,
   Old Time is still a-flying:
And this same flower that smiles to-day
   To-morrow will be dying.

The glorious lamp of heaven, the sun,
   The higher he's a-getting,
The sooner will his race be run,
   And nearer he's to setting.

That age is best which is the first,
   When youth and blood are warmer;

But being spent, the worse, and worst
  Times still succeed the former.

Then be not coy, but use your time,
  And while ye may, go marry:
For having lost but once your prime,
  You may for ever tarry.

Upon Julia's Clothes

Whenas in silks my Julia goes,
Then, then, methinks, how sweetly flows
The liquefaction of her clothes!

Next, when I cast mine eyes and see
That brave vibration each way free,
—O how that glittering taketh me!

Chop-Cherry

Thou gav'st me leave to kiss,
  Thou gav'st me leave to woo;
Thou mad'st me think, by this
  And that, thou lov'st me too.

But I shall ne'er forget
  How, for to make thee merry
Thou mad'st me chop, but yet
  Another snapp'd the cherry.

FRANCIS QUARLES
(1592–1644)

A Divine Rapture

E'en like two little bank-dividing brooks,
   That wash the pebbles with their wanton streams,
And having ranged and search'd a thousand nooks,
   Meet both at length in silver-breasted Thames,
     Where in a greater current they conjoin:
So I my Best-beloved's am; so He is mine.

E'en so we met; and after long pursuit,
   E'en so we joined; we both became entire;
No need for either to renew a suit,
   For I was flax, and He was flames of fire:
     Our firm-united souls did more than twine;
So I my Best-beloved's am; so He is mine.

If all those glittering Monarchs, that command
   The servile quarters of this earthly ball,
Should tender in exchange their shares of land,
   I would not change my fortunes for them all:
     Their wealth is but a counter to my coin:
The world's but theirs; but my Beloved's mine.

HENRY KING
(1592–1669)

Sonnet

Tell me no more how fair she is,
   I have no mind to hear
The story of that distant bliss
   I never shall come near:
By sad experience I have found
That her perfection is my wound.

And tell me not how fond I am
    To tempt a daring Fate,
From whence no triumph ever came,
    But to repent too late:
There is some hope ere long I may
In silence dote my self away.

I ask no pity (Love) from thee,
    Nor will thy justice blame,
So that thou wilt not envy me
    The glory of my flame:
Which crowns my heart whene'er it dies,
In that it falls her sacrifice.

Exequy on His Wife

Accept, thou shrine of my dead saint,
Instead of dirges this complaint;
And for sweet flowers to crown thy hearse,
Receive a strew of weeping verse
From thy grieved friend, whom thou mightst see
Quite melted into tears for thee.
    Dear loss! since thy untimely fate
My task hath been to meditate
On thee, on thee! Thou art the book,
The library, whereon I look
Though almost blind. For thee, loved clay,
I languish out, not live, the day,
Using no other exercise
But what I practise with mine eyes.
By which wet glasses I find out
How lazily time creeps about
To one that mourns. This, only this,
My exercise and business is:
So I compute the weary hours
With sighs dissolved into showers.
    Nor wonder if my time go thus
Backward and most preposterous:

Thou hast benighted me; thy set
This eve of blackness did beget,
Who wast my day (though overcast
Before thou hadst thy noontide past)
And I remember must in tears
Thou scarce hadst seen so many years
As day tells hours. By thy clear sun
My love and fortune first did run;
But thou wilt never more appear
Folded within my hemisphere,
Since both thy light and motion,
Like a fled star, is fallen and gone,
And 'twixt me and my soul's dear wish
The earth now interposed is,
Which such a strange eclipse doth make
As ne'er was read in almanac.

　I could allow thee for a time
To darken me and my sad clime;
Were it a month, a year, or ten,
I would thy exile live till then,
And all that space my mirth adjourn—
So thou wouldst promise to return
And, putting off thy ashy shroud,
At length disperse this sorrow's cloud.

　But woe is me! the longest date
Too narrow is to calculate
These empty hopes. Never shall I
Be so much blessed as to descry
A glimpse of thee, till that day come
Which shall the earth to cinders doom,
And a fierce fever must calcine
The body of this world, like thine,
My little world! That fit of fire
Once off, our bodies shall aspire
To our souls' bliss: then we shall rise
And view ourselves with clearer eyes
In that calm region where no night
Can hide us from each other's sight.

　Meantime thou hast her, Earth: much good
May my harm do thee. Since it stood
With Heaven's will I might not call

Her longer mine, I give thee all
My short-lived right and interest
In her, whom living I loved best:
With a most free and bounteous grief,
I give thee what I could not keep.
Be kind to her, and prithee look
Thou write into thy Doomsday book
Each parcel of this rarity,
Which in thy casket shrined doth lie.
See that thou make thy reckoning straight,
And yield her back again by weight;
For thou must audit on thy trust
Each grain and atom of this dust,
As thou wilt answer him that lent,
Not gave thee, my dear monument.
    So close the ground, and 'bout her shade
Black curtains draw: my bride is laid.
    Sleep on, my Love, in thy cold bed
Never to be disquieted.
My last good night! Thou wilt not wake
Till I thy fate shall overtake:
Till age, or grief, or sickness must
Marry my body to that dust
It so much loves; and fill the room
My heart keeps empty in thy tomb.
Stay for me there: I will not fail
To meet thee in that hollow vale.
And think not much of my delay;
I am already on the way,
And follow thee with all the speed
Desire can make, or sorrows breed.
Each minute is a short degree
And every hour a step towards thee.
At night when I betake to rest,
Next morn I rise nearer my west
Of life, almost by eight hours sail
Than when sleep breathed his drowsy gale.
    Thus from the sun my bottom steers,
And my day's compass downward bears.
Nor labour I to stem the tide
Through which to thee I swiftly glide.

'Tis true, with shame and grief I yield;
Thou, like the van, first took'st the field
And gotten hast the victory
In thus adventuring to die
Before me, whose more years might crave
A just precedence in the grave.
But hark! my pulse, like a soft drum,
Beats my approach, tells thee I come;
And slow howe'er my marches be
I shall at last sit down by thee.
　The thought of this bids me go on
And wait my dissolution
With hope and comfort. Dear—forgive
The crime—I am content to live
Divided, with but half a heart,
Till we shall meet and never part.

THOMAS CAREW
(1595?–1645?)

Song

Ask me no more where Jove bestows,
When June is past, the fading rose;
For in your beauty's orient deep
These flowers, as in their causes, sleep.

Ask me no more whither do stray
The golden atoms of the day;
For in pure love heaven did prepare
Those powders to enrich your hair.

Ask me no more whither doth haste
The nightingale when May is past;
For in your sweet dividing throat
She winters and keeps warm her note.

Ask me no more where those stars 'light
That downwards fall in dead of night;

For in your eyes they sit, and there
Fixed become as in their sphere.

Ask me no more if east or west
The Phoenix builds her spicy nest;
For unto you at last she flies,
And in your fragrant bosom dies.

To His Inconstant Mistress

When thou, poor Excommunicate
    From all the joys of Love, shalt see
The full reward and glorious fate
    Which my strong faith shall purchase me,
    Then curse thine own inconstancy!

A fairer hand than thine shall cure
    That heart which thy false oaths did wound;
And to my soul a soul more pure
    Than thine shall by Love's hand be bound,
    And both with equal glory crown'd.

Then shalt thou weep, entreat, complain
    To Love, as I did once to thee;
When all thy tears shall be as vain
    As mine were then: for thou shalt be
    Damn'd for thy false apostasy.

EDMUND WALLER
(1606–1687)

On a Girdle

That which her slender waist confined
Shall now my joyful temples bind;
No monarch but would give his crown
His arms might do what this has done.

It was my Heaven's extremest sphere,
The pale which held that lovely deer:
My joy, my grief, my hope, my love,
Did all within this circle move.

A narrow compass! and yet there
Dwelt all that's good, and all that's fair!
Give me but what this ribband bound,
Take all the rest the sun goes round!

Song

Go, lovely Rose—
Tell her that wastes her time and me,
That now she knows,
When I resemble her to thee,
How sweet and fair she seems to be.

Tell her that's young,
And shuns to have her graces spied,
That hadst thou sprung
In deserts where no men abide,
Thou must have uncommended died.

Small is the worth
Of beauty from the light retired:
Bid her come forth,
Suffer herself to be desired,
And not blush so to be admired.

Then die—that she
The common fate of all things rare
May read in thee;
How small a part of time they share
That are so wondrous sweet and fair!

JOHN MILTON
(1608–1674)

On His Deceased Wife

Methought I saw my late espoused Saint
  Brought to me like Alcestis from the grave,
  Whom Jove's great Son to her glad Husband gave,
  Rescu'd from death by force though pale and faint,
Mine as whom washt from spot of child-bed taint,
  Purification in the old Law did save,
  And such, as yet once more I trust to have
Full sight of her in Heaven without restraint,
Came vested all in white, pure as her mind:
  Her face was vail'd, yet to my fancied sight,
  Love, sweetness, goodness, in her person shin'd
So clear, as in no face with more delight.
  But O as to embrace me she enclin'd
  I wak'd, she fled, and day brought back my night.

SIR JOHN SUCKLING
(1609–1642)

'Why So Pale and Wan, Fond Lover?'

Why so pale and wan, fond lover?
    Prithee, why so pale?
Will, when looking well can't move her,
    Looking ill prevail?
    Prithee, why so pale?

Why so dull and mute, young sinner?
    Prithee, why so mute?
Will, when speaking well can't win her,
    Saying nothing do 't?
    Prithee, why so mute?

Quit, quit for shame! This will not move;
   This cannot take her.
If of herself she will not love,
     Nothing can make her:
     The devil take her!

The Constant Lover

Out upon it, I have loved
   Three whole days together!
And am like to love three more,
   If it prove fair weather.

Time shall moult away his wings
   Ere he shall discover
In the whole wide world again
   Such a constant lover.

But the spite on 't is, no praise
   Is due at all to me:
Love with me had made no stays,
   Had it any been but she.

Had it any been but she,
   And that very face,
There had been at least ere this
   A dozen dozen in her place.

RICHARD LOVELACE
(1618–1658)

To Lucasta, Going to the Wars

Tell me not, Sweet, I am unkind,
   That from the nunnery
Of thy chaste breast and quiet mind
   To war and arms I fly.

True, a new mistress now I chase,
    The first foe in the field;
And with a stronger faith embrace
    A sword, a horse, a shield.

Yet this inconstancy is such
    As thou too shalt adore;
I could not love thee, Dear, so much,
    Loved I not Honour more.

To Althea, from Prison

When Love with unconfined wings
    Hovers within my gates,
And my divine Althea brings
    To whisper at the grates;
When I lie tangled in her hair
    And fetter'd to her eye,
The birds that wanton in the air
    Know no such liberty.

When flowing cups run swiftly round
    With no allaying Thames,
Our careless heads with roses bound,
    Our hearts with loyal flames;
When thirsty grief in wine we steep,
    When healths and draughts go free—
Fishes that tipple in the deep
    Know no such liberty.

When, like committed linnets, I
    With shriller throat shall sing
The sweetness, mercy, majesty,
    And glories of my King;
When I shall voice aloud how good
    He is, how great should be,
Enlarged winds, that curl the flood,
    Know no such liberty.

Stone walls do not a prison make,
    Nor iron bars a cage;
Minds innocent and quiet take
    That for an hermitage;
If I have freedom in my love
    And in my soul am free,
Angels alone, that soar above,
    Enjoy such liberty.

The Scrutiny

Why should you swear I am forsworn,
    Since thine I vow'd to be?
Lady it is already morn,
    And 'twas last night I swore to thee
That fond impossibility.

Have I not lov'd thee much and long,
    A tedious twelve hours space?
I must all other beauties wrong,
    And rob thee of a new embrace,
Could I still dote upon thy face.

Not, but all joy in thy brown hair,
    By others may be found;
But I must search the black and fair
    Like skilfull mineralists that sound
For treasure in unplow'd-up ground.

Then, if when I have lov'd my round,
    Thou prov'st the pleasant she;
With spoils of meaner beauties crown'd,
    I laden will return to thee,
Ev'n sated with variety.

ANDREW MARVELL
(1621–1678)

To His Coy Mistress

Had we but world enough, and time,
This coyness, Lady, were no crime.
We would sit down and think which way
To walk and pass our long love's day.
Thou by the Indian Ganges' side
Shouldst rubies find: I by the tide
Of Humber would complain. I would
Love you ten years before the Flood,
And you should, if you please, refuse
Till the conversion of the Jews.
My vegetable love should grow
Vaster than empires, and more slow;
An hundred years should go to praise
Thine eyes and on thy forehead gaze;
Two hundred to adore each breast;
But thirty thousand to the rest;
An age at least to every part,
And the last age should show your heart;
For, Lady, you deserve this state,
Nor would I love at lower rate.
    But at my back I always hear
Time's winged chariot hurrying near;
And yonder all before us lie
Deserts of vast eternity.
Thy beauty shall no more be found,
Nor, in thy marble vault, shall sound
My echoing song: then worms shall try
That long preserved virginity,
And your quaint honour turn to dust,
And into ashes all my lust:
The grave's a fine and private place,
But none, I think, do there embrace.
    Now therefore, while the youthful hue
Sits on thy skin like morning dew,

And while thy willing soul transpires
At every pore with instant fires,
Now let us sport us while we may,
And now, like amorous birds of prey,
Rather at once our time devour
Than languish in his slow-chapt[1] power.
Let us roll all our strength and all
Our sweetness up into one ball,
And tear our pleasures with rough strife
Thorough the iron gates of life:
Thus, though we cannot make our sun
Stand still, yet we will make him run.

[1] *slow-chapt*] slowly devouring.

The Definition of Love

My Love is of a birth as rare
As 'tis for object strange and high:
It was begotten by Despair
Upon Impossibility.

Magnanimous Despair alone
Could show me so divine a thing,
Where feeble Hope could ne'r have flown
But vainly flapt its tinsel wing.

And yet I quickly might arrive
Where my extended Soul is fixt,
But Fate does iron wedges drive,
And always crowds it self betwixt.

For Fate with jealous eye does see
Two perfect Loves; nor lets them close:
Their union would her ruin be,
And her Tyrannic pow'r depose.

And therefore her Decrees of Steel
Us as the distant Poles have plac'd,
(Though Love's whole World on us doth wheel)
Not by themselves to be embrac'd.

Unless the giddy Heaven fall,
And Earth some new Convulsion tear;
And, us to join, the World should all
Be cramp'd into a *Planisphere*.

As Lines so Loves *oblique* may well
Themselves in every Angle greet:
But ours so truly *Parallel*,
Though infinite can never meet.

Therefore the Love which us doth bind
But Fate so enviously debars,
Is the Conjunction of the Mind,
And Opposition of the Stars.

The Mower to the Glo-Worms

Ye living Lamps, by whose dear light
The Nightingale does sit so late,
And studying all the Summer-night,
Her matchless Songs does meditate;

Ye Country Comets, that portend
No War, nor Princes funeral,
Shining unto no higher end
Than to presage the Grasses fall;

Ye Glo-worms, whose officious Flame
To wandring Mowers shows the way,
That in the Night have lost their aim,
And after foolish Fires do stray;

Your courteous Lights in vain you waste,
Since *Juliana* here is come,
For She my Mind hath so displac'd
That I shall never find my home.

JOHN DRYDEN
(1631–1700)

'Farewell, Ungrateful Traitor!'

Farewell, ungrateful traitor!
   Farewell, my perjur'd swain!
Let never injur'd creature
   Believe a man again.
The pleasure of possessing
Surpasses all expressing,
But 't is too short a blessing,
   And love too long a pain.

'T is easy to deceive us,
   In pity of your pain;
But when we love, you leave us
   To rail at you in vain.
Before we have descried it,
There is no bliss beside it;
But she that once has tried it,
   Will never love again.

The passion you pretended,
   Was only to obtain;
But when the charm is ended,
   The charmer you disdain.
Your love by ours we measure,
Till we have lost our treasure;
But dying is a pleasure,
   When living is a pain.

JOHN WILMOT, EARL OF ROCHESTER
(1647–1680)

Return

Absent from thee, I languish still;
   Then ask me not, When I return?
The straying fool 'twill plainly kill
   To wish all day, all night to mourn.

Dear, from thine arms then let me fly,
   That my fantastic mind may prove
The torments it deserves to try,
   That tears my fix'd heart from my love.

When, wearied with a world of woe,
   To thy safe bosom I retire,
Where love, and peace, and truth does flow,
   May I contented there expire!

Lest, once more wandering from that heaven,
   I fall on some base heart unblest;
Faithless to thee, false, unforgiven—
   And lose my everlasting rest.

A Song of a Young Lady to Her Ancient Lover

Ancient person, for whom I
All the flattering youth defy,
Long be it ere thou grow old,
Aching, shaking, crazy, cold;
   But still continue as thou art,
   Ancient person of my heart.

On thy withered lips and dry,
Which like barren furrows lie,
Brooding kisses I will pour
Shall thy youthful heat restore

(Such kind showers in autumn fall,
And a second spring recall);
   Nor from thee will ever part,
   Ancient person of my heart.

The nobler part, which but to name
In our sex would be counted shame,
By age's frozen grasp possessed,
From his ice shall be released,
And soothed by my reviving hand,
In former warmth and vigour stand.
All a lover's wish can reach
For thy joy my love shall teach,
And for thy pleasure shall improve
All that art can add to love.
   Yet still I love thee without art,
   Ancient person of my heart.

MATTHEW PRIOR

(1664–1721)

An Ode

The merchant, to secure his treasure,
   Conveys it in a borrowed name;
Euphelia serves to grace my measure,
   But Cloe is my real flame.

My softest verse, my darling lyre,
   Upon Euphelia's toilet lay;
When Cloe noted her desire
   That I should sing, that I should play.

My lyre I tune, my voice I raise,
   But with my numbers mix my sighs;
And whilst I sing Euphelia's praise,
   I fix my soul on Cloe's eyes.

Fair Cloe blushed; Euphelia frowned;
   I sung and gazed; I played and trembled;
And Venus to the Loves around
   Remarked how ill we all dissembled.

WILLIAM CONGREVE
(1670–1729)

'Pious Selinda Goes to Prayers'

Pious Selinda goes to prayers,
   If I but ask the favour;
And yet the tender fool's in tears,
   When she believes I'll leave her.

Would I were free from this restraint,
   Or else had hopes to win her;
Would she could make of me a saint,
   Or I of her a sinner.

'False though She Be to Me and Love'

False though she be to me and love,
   I'll ne'er pursue revenge;
For still the charmer I approve,
   Though I deplore her change.

In hours of bliss we oft have met;
   They could not always last;
And though the present I regret,
   I'm grateful for the past.

JOHN GAY
(1685–1732)

Sweet William's Farewell to Black-Eyed Susan

All in the Downs the fleet was moored,
 The streamers waving in the wind,
When black-eyed Susan came aboard,
  'Oh! where shall I my true love find?
Tell me, ye jovial sailors, tell me true,
If my sweet William sails among the crew.'

William, who high upon the yard,
 Rocked with the billow to and fro,
Soon as her well-known voice he heard,
  He sighed, and cast his eyes below;
The cord slides swiftly through his glowing hands
And, quick as lightning, on the deck he stands.

So the sweet lark, high-poised in air,
 Shuts close his pinions to his breast,
If, chance, his mate's shrill call he hear
  And drops at once into her nest.
The noblest captain in the British fleet,
Might envy William's lip those kisses sweet.

'O Susan, Susan, lovely dear,
 My vows shall ever true remain;
Let me kiss off that falling tear,
  We only part to meet again.
Change, as ye list, ye winds; my heart shall be
The faithful compass that still points to thee.

Believe not what the landsmen say,
 Who tempt with doubts thy constant mind;
They'll tell thee, sailors, when away,
  In every port a mistress find.
Yes, yes, believe them when they tell thee so,
For thou art present whereso'er I go.

If to far India's coast we sail,
 Thy eyes are seen in diamonds bright,

Thy breath is Afric's spicy gale,
  Thy skin is ivory, so white.
Thus every beauteous object that I view,
Wakes in my soul some charm of lovely Sue.

Though battle call me from thy arms,
  Let not my pretty Susan mourn;
Though cannons roar, yet safe from harms,
  William shall to his dear return.
Love turns aside the balls that round me fly,
Lest precious tears should drop from Susan's eye.'

The boatswain gave the dreadful word,
  The sails their swelling bosom spread,
No longer must she stay aboard;
  They kissed, she sighed, he hung his head.
Her lessening boat unwilling rows to land:
'Adieu,' she cries, and waved her lily hand.

HENRY CAREY

(1687?–1743)

Sally in Our Alley

Of all the girls that are so smart
  There's none like pretty Sally;
She is the darling of my heart,
  And she lives in our alley.
There is no lady in the land
  Is half so sweet as Sally;
She is the darling of my heart,
  And she lives in our alley.

Her father he makes cabbage-nets,
  And through the streets does cry 'em;
Her mother she sells laces long
  To such as please to buy 'em:
But sure such folks could ne'er beget
  So sweet a girl as Sally!

She is the darling of my heart,
   And she lives in our alley.

When she is by, I leave my work,
   I love her so sincerely;
My master comes like any Turk,
   And bangs me most severely:
But let him bang his bellyful,
   I'll bear it all for Sally;
She is the darling of my heart,
   And she lives in our alley.

Of all the days that's in the week
   I dearly love but one day—
And that's the day that comes betwixt
   A Saturday and Monday;
For then I'm dressed all in my best
   To walk abroad with Sally;
She is the darling of my heart,
   And she lives in our alley.

My master carries me to church,
   And often am I blamed
Because I leave him in the lurch
   As soon as text is named;
I leave the church in sermon-time
   And slink away to Sally;
She is the darling of my heart,
   And she lives in our alley.

When Christmas comes about again,
   O, then I shall have money;
I'll hoard it up, and box it all,
   I'll give it to my honey:
I would it were ten thousand pound,
   I'd give it all to Sally;
She is the darling of my heart,
   And she lives in our alley.

My master and the neighbours all
   Make game of me and Sally,
And, but for her, I'd better be
   A slave and row a galley;

But when my seven long years are out,
O, then I'll marry Sally;
O, then we'll wed, and then we'll bed—
But not in our alley!

WILLIAM COWPER
(1731–1800)

To Mary

The twentieth year is well-nigh past,
Since first our sky was overcast;
Ah would that this might be the last!
My Mary!

Thy spirits have a fainter flow,
I see thee daily weaker grow—
'Twas my distress that brought thee low,
My Mary!

Thy needles, once a shining store,
For my sake restless heretofore,
Now rust disus'd, and shine no more,
My Mary!

For though thou gladly wouldst fulfil
The same kind office for me still,
Thy sight now seconds not thy will,
My Mary!

But well thou play'dst the housewife's part,
And all thy threads with magic art
Have wound themselves about this heart,
My Mary!

Thy indistinct expressions seem
Like language utter'd in a dream;
Yet me they charm, whate'er the theme,
My Mary!

Thy silver locks, once auburn bright,
Are still more lovely in my sight
Than golden beams of orient light,
           My Mary!

For could I view nor them nor thee,
What sight worth seeing could I see?
The sun would rise in vain for me,
           My Mary!

Partakers of thy sad decline,
Thy hands their little force resign;
Yet, gently prest, press gently mine,
           My Mary!

And then I feel that still I hold
A richer store ten thousandfold
Than misers fancy in their gold,
           My Mary!

Such feebleness of limbs thou prov'st,
That now at every step thou mov'st
Upheld by two; yet still thou lov'st,
           My Mary!

And still to love, though prest with ill,
In wintry age to feel no chill,
With me is to be lovely still,
           My Mary!

But ah! by constant heed I know,
How oft the sadness that I show
Transforms thy smiles to looks of woe,
           My Mary!

And should my future lot be cast
With much resemblance of the past,
Thy worn-out heart will break at last.
           My Mary!

WILLIAM BLAKE
(1757–1827)

'How Sweet I Roam'd from Field to Field'

How sweet I roam'd from field to field
And tasted all the summer's pride,
Till I the Prince of Love beheld
Who in the sunny beams did glide!

He show'd me lilies for my hair,
And blushing roses for my brow;
He led me through his gardens fair
Where all his golden pleasures grow.

With sweet May dews my wings were wet,
And Phoebus fir'd my vocal rage;
He caught me in his silken net,
And shut me in his golden cage.

He loves to sit and hear me sing,
Then, laughing, sports and plays with me;
Then stretches out my golden wing,
And mocks my loss of liberty.

Love's Secret

Never seek to tell thy love,
    Love that never told can be;
For the gentle wind doth move
    Silently, invisibly.

I told my love, I told my love,
    I told her all my heart,
Trembling, cold, in ghastly fears.
    Ah! she did depart!

Soon after she was gone from me,
    A traveller came by,
Silently, invisibly:
    He took her with a sigh.

The Clod and the Pebble

"Love seeketh not Itself to please,
"Nor for itself hath any care,
"But for another gives its ease,
"And builds a Heaven in Hell's despair."

So sang a little Clod of Clay
Trodden with the cattle's feet,
But a Pebble of the brook
Warbled out these metres meet:

"Love seeketh only Self to please,
"To bind another to Its delight,
"Joys in another's loss of ease,
"And builds a Hell in Heaven's despite."

The Garden of Love

I went to the Garden of Love,
And saw what I never had seen:
A Chapel was built in the midst,
Where I used to play on the green.

And the gates of this Chapel were shut,
And "Thou shalt not" writ over the door;
So I turn'd to the Garden of Love
That so many sweet flowers bore;

And I saw it was filled with graves,
And tomb-stones where flowers should be;
And Priests in black gowns were walking their rounds,
And binding with briars my joys & desires.

ROBERT BURNS
(1759–1796)

'Of A' the Airts the Wind Can Blaw'

Of a' the airts[1] the wind can blaw
   I dearly like the west,
For there the bonie lassie lives,
   The lassie I lo'e best.
There wild woods grow, and rivers row,[2]
   And monie a hill between,
But day and night my fancy's flight
   Is ever wi' my Jean.

I see her in the dewy flowers—
   I see her sweet and fair.
I hear her in the tunefu' birds—
   I hear her charm the air.
There's not a bonie flower that springs
   By fountain, shaw,[3] or green,
There's not a bonie bird that sings,
   But minds me o' my Jean.

[1] *airts*] directions.
[2] *row*] roll.
[3] *shaw*] wood.

John Anderson My Jo

John Anderson my jo, John,
   When we were first acquent,[1]
Your locks were like the raven,
   Your bonie brow was brent;[2]

But now your brow is beld,[3] John,
   Your locks are like the snaw,[4]
But blessings on your frosty pow,[5]
   John Anderson my jo!

John Anderson my jo, John,
   We clamb the hill thegither,
And monie a cantie[6] day, John,
   We've had wi' ane anither;
Now we maun totter down, John,
   And hand in hand we'll go,
And sleep thegither at the foot,
   John Anderson my jo!

[1] *acquent*] acquainted.
[2] *brent*] not sloping through baldness.
[3] *beld*] bald.
[4] *snaw*] snow.
[5] *pow*] poll, head.
[6] *cantie*] cheerful.

The Banks o' Doon

Ye banks and braes[1] o' bonie Doon,
   How can ye bloom sae fresh and fair?
How can ye chant, ye little birds,
   And I sae weary fu' o' care!
Thou'll break my heart, thou warbling bird,
   That wantons thro' the flowering thorn!
Thou minds me o' departed joys,
   Departed never to return.

Aft hae I rov'd by bonie Doon
   To see the rose and woodbine twine,
And ilka[2] bird sang o' its luve,
   And fondly sae did I o' mine.

Wi' lightsome heart I pu'd a rose,
  Fu' sweet upon its thorny tree!
And my fause luver staw[3] my rose—
  But ah! he left the thorn wi' me.

---

[1] *braes*] small hills, slopes.
[2] *ilka*] every.
[3] *staw*] stole.

A Red, Red Rose

O, my luve is like a red, red rose,
  That's newly sprung in June.
O, my luve is like the melodie,
  That's sweetly play'd in tune.

As fair art thou, my bonie lass,
  So deep in luve am I,
And I will luve thee still, my dear,
  Till a' the seas gang dry.

Till a' the seas gang dry, my dear,
  And the rocks melt wi' the sun!
And I will luve thee still, my dear,
  While the sands o' life shall run.

And fare thee weel, my only luve,
  And fare thee weel a while!
And I will come again, my luve,
  Tho' it were ten thousand mile!

WILLIAM WORDSWORTH
(1770–1850)

'Strange Fits of Passion Have I Known'

Strange fits of passion have I known:
And I will dare to tell,
But in the Lover's ear alone,
What once to me befell.

When she I loved looked every day
Fresh as a rose in June,
I to her cottage bent my way,
Beneath an evening-moon.

Upon the moon I fixed my eye,
All over the wide lea;
With quickening pace my horse drew nigh
Those paths so dear to me.

And now we reached the orchard-plot;
And, as we climbed the hill,
The sinking moon to Lucy's cot
Came near, and nearer still.

In one of those sweet dreams I slept,
Kind Nature's gentlest boon!
And all the while my eyes I kept
On the descending moon.

My horse moved on; hoof after hoof
He raised, and never stopped:
When down behind the cottage roof,
At once, the bright moon dropped.

What fond and wayward thoughts will slide
Into a Lover's head!
"O mercy!" to myself I cried,
"If Lucy should be dead!"

'She Dwelt among the Untrodden Ways'

She dwelt among the untrodden ways
    Beside the springs of Dove,
A Maid whom there were none to praise
    And very few to love:

A violet by a mossy stone
    Half hidden from the eye!
—Fair as a star, when only one
    Is shining in the sky.

She lived unknown, and few could know
    When Lucy ceased to be;
But she is in her grave, and, oh,
    The difference to me!

'Surprised by Joy—Impatient as the Wind'

Surprised by joy—impatient as the wind
    I turned to share the transport—O! with whom
    But Thee, deep buried in the silent tomb,
That spot which no vicissitude can find?
Love, faithful love, recalled thee to my mind—
    But how could I forget thee? Through what power,
    Even for the least division of an hour,
Have I been so beguiled as to be blind
To my most grievous loss?—That thought's return
    Was the worst pang that sorrow ever bore,
Save one, one only, when I stood forlorn,
    Knowing my heart's best treasure was no more;
That neither present time, nor years unborn
    Could to my sight that heavenly face restore.

SIR WALTER SCOTT
(1771–1832)

An Hour with Thee

An hour with thee! When earliest day
Dapples with gold the eastern grey,
Oh, what can frame my mind to bear
The toil and turmoil, cark and care,
New griefs, which coming hours unfold,
And sad remembrance of the old?
   One hour with thee.

One hour with thee! When burning June
Waves his red flag at pitch of noon;
What shall repay the faithful swain,
His labour on the sultry plain;
And, more than cave or sheltering bough,
Cool feverish blood and throbbing brow?
   One hour with thee.

One hour with thee! When sun is set,
Oh, what can teach me to forget
The thankless labours of the day;
The hopes, the wishes, flung away;
The increasing wants, and lessening gains,
The master's pride, who scorns my pains?
   One hour with thee.

WALTER SAVAGE LANDOR
(1775–1864)

'Past Ruin'd Ilion Helen Lives'

Past ruin'd Ilion Helen lives,
 Alcestis rises from the shades;
Verse calls them forth; 'tis verse that gives
 Immortal youth to mortal maids.

Soon shall Oblivion's deepening veil
    Hide all the peopled hills you see,
The gay, the proud, while lovers hail
    These many summers you and me.

'Proud Word You Never Spoke, but You Will Speak'

Proud word you never spoke, but you will speak
    Four not exempt from pride some future day.
Resting on one white hand a warm wet cheek,
    Over my open volume you will say,
'This man loved *me*'—then rise and trip away.

Rose Aylmer

Ah, what avails the sceptred race!
    Ah, what the form divine!
What every virtue, every grace!
    Rose Aylmer, all were thine.

Rose Aylmer, whom these wakeful eyes
    May weep, but never see,
A night of memories and sighs
    I consecrate to thee.

'You Smiled, You Spoke, and I Believed'

You smiled, you spoke, and I believed,
By every word and smile deceived.
Another man would hope no more;
Nor hope I what I hoped before:
But let not this last wish be vain;
Deceive, deceive me once again!

'The Torch of Love Dispels the Gloom'

The torch of Love dispels the gloom
Of life, and animates the tomb;
But never let it idly flare
On gazers in the open air,
Nor turn it quite away from one
To whom it serves for moon and sun,
And who alike in night or day
Without it could not find his way.

'If I Am Proud, You Surely Know'

If I am proud, you surely know,
Ianthe! who has made me so,
And only should condemn the pride
That can arise from aught beside.

THOMAS CAMPBELL
(1777–1844)

Freedom and Love

How delicious is the winning
Of a kiss at love's beginning,
When two mutual hearts are sighing
For the knot there's no untying!

Yet remember, 'midst your wooing
Love has bliss, but Love has ruing;
Other smiles may make you fickle,
Tears for other charms may trickle.

Love he comes and Love he tarries
Just as fate or fancy carries;
Longest stays, when sorest chidden;
Laughs and flies, when press'd and bidden.

Bind the sea to slumber stilly,
Bind its odour to the lily,
Bind the aspen ne'er to quiver,
Then bind Love to last for ever.

Love's a fire that needs renewal
Of fresh beauty for its fuel:
Love's wing moults when caged and captured,
Only free, he soars enraptured.

Can you keep the bee from ranging,
Or the ringdove's neck from changing?
No! nor fetter'd Love from dying
In the knot there's no untying.

THOMAS MOORE

(1779–1852)

Did Not

'Twas a new feeling—something more
Than we had dared to own before,
    Which then we hid not;
We saw it in each other's eye,
And wished, in every half-breathed sigh,
    To speak, but did not.

She felt my lips' impassioned touch—
'Twas the first time I dared so much,
    And yet she chid not;
But whispered o'er my burning brow,
'Oh, do you doubt I love you now?'
    Sweet soul! I did not.

Warmly I felt her bosom thrill,
I pressed it closer, closer still,
   Though gently bid not;
Till—oh! the world hath seldom heard
Of lovers, who so nearly erred,
   And yet, who did not.

An Argument

I've oft been told by learned friars,
   That wishing and the crime are one,
And Heaven punishes desires
   As much as if the deed were done.

If wishing damns us, you and I
   Are damned to all our heart's content;
Come, then, at least we may enjoy
   Some pleasure for our punishment!

At the Mid Hour of Night

At the mid hour of night, when stars are weeping, I fly
To the lone vale we loved, when life shone warm in thine eye;
   And I think oft, if spirits can steal from the regions of air
   To revisit past scenes of delight, thou wilt come to me there,
And tell me our love is remember'd even in the sky.

Then I sing the wild song it once was rapture to hear,
When our voices commingling breathed like one on the ear;
   And as Echo far off through the vale my sad orison rolls,
   I think, O my love! 'tis thy voice from the Kingdom of Souls
Faintly answering still the notes that once were so dear.

GEORGE GORDON, LORD BYRON
(1788–1824)

'When We Two Parted'

When we two parted
In silence and tears,
Half broken-hearted,
To sever for years,
Pale grew thy cheek and cold,
Colder thy kiss;
Truly that hour foretold
Sorrow to this!

The dew of the morning
Sunk chill on my brow;
It felt like the warning
Of what I feel now.
Thy vows are all broken,
And light is thy fame:
I hear thy name spoken
And share in its shame.

They name thee before me,
A knell to mine ear;
A shudder comes o'er me—
Why wert thou so dear?
They know not I knew thee
Who knew thee too well:
Long, long shall I rue thee
Too deeply to tell.

In secret we met:
In silence I grieve
That thy heart could forget,
Thy spirit deceive.
If I should meet thee

After long years,
How should I greet thee?—
With silence and tears.

'She Walks in Beauty, Like the Night'

She walks in beauty, like the night
  Of cloudless climes and starry skies;
And all that's best of dark and bright
  Meet in her aspect and her eyes:
Thus mellowed to that tender light
  Which heaven to gaudy day denies.

One shade the more, one ray the less,
  Had half impaired the nameless grace
Which waves in every raven tress
  Or softly lightens o'er her face;
Where thoughts serenely sweet express
  How pure, how dear their dwelling-place.

And on that cheek, and o'er that brow
  So soft, so calm, yet eloquent,
The smiles that win, the tints that glow,
  But tell of days in goodness spent,
A mind at peace with all below,
  A heart whose love is innocent!

'So, We'll Go No More A-Roving'

So, we'll go no more a-roving
  So late into the night,
Though the heart be still as loving,
  And the moon be still as bright.

For the sword outwears its sheath,
  And the soul wears out the breast,
And the heart must pause to breathe,
  And love itself have rest.

Though the night was made for loving,
   And the day returns too soon,
Yet we'll go no more a-roving
   By the light of the moon.

PERCY BYSSHE SHELLEY
(1792–1822)

Love's Philosophy

The fountains mingle with the river
   And the rivers with the Ocean,
The winds of Heaven mix for ever
   With a sweet emotion;
Nothing in the world is single;
   All things by a law divine
In one spirit meet and mingle.
   Why not I with thine?—

See the mountains kiss high Heaven
   And the waves clasp one another;
No sister-flower would be forgiven
   If it disdained its brother;
And the sunlight clasps the earth
   And the moonbeams kiss the sea:
What is all this sweet work worth
   If thou kiss not me?

To——

One word is too often profaned
   For me to profane it,
One feeling too falsely disdained
   For thee to disdain it;
One hope is too like despair

For prudence to smother,
And pity from thee more dear
  Than that from another.

I can give not what men call love,
  But wilt thou accept not
The worship the heart lifts above
  And the Heavens reject not,—
The desire of the moth for the star,
  Of the night for the morrow,
The devotion to something afar
  From the sphere of our sorrow?

JOHN CLARE
(1793–1864)

First Love

I ne'er was struck before that hour
  With love so sudden and so sweet,
Her face it bloomed like a sweet flower
  And stole my heart away complete.
My face turned pale as deadly pale.
  My legs refused to walk away,
And when she looked, what could I ail?
  My life and all seemed turned to clay.

And then my blood rushed to my face
  And took my eyesight quite away,
The trees and bushes round the place
  Seemed midnight at noonday.
I could not see a single thing,
  Words from my eyes did start—
They spoke as chords do from the string,
  And blood burnt round my heart.

Are flowers the winter's choice?
  Is love's bed always snow?
She seemed to hear my silent voice,

Not love's appeals to know.
I never saw so sweet a face
    As that I stood before.
My heart has left its dwelling-place
    And can return no more.

To Mary: 'It Is the Evening Hour'

It is the evening hour,
    How silent all doth lie:
The horned moon she shows her face
    In the river with the sky.
Just by the path on which we pass,
    The flaggy lake lies still as glass.

Spirit of her I love,
    Whispering to me
Stories of sweet visions as I rove,
    Here stop, and crop with me
Sweet flowers that in the still hour grew,
We'll take them home, nor shake off the bright dew.

Mary, or sweet spirit of thee,
    As the bright sun shines to-morrow
Thy dark eyes these flowers shall see,
    Gathered by me in sorrow,
Into the still hour when my mind was free
To walk alone—yet wish I walked with thee.

To Mary: 'I Sleep with Thee, and Wake with Thee'

I sleep with thee, and wake with thee,
    And yet thou art not there;
I fill my arms with thoughts of thee,
    And press the common air.

Thy eyes are gazing upon mine,
   When thou art out of sight;
My lips are always touching thine,
   At morning, noon, and night.

I think and speak of other things
   To keep my mind at rest:
But still to thee my memory clings
   Like love in woman's breast.
I hide it from the world's wide eye,
   And think and speak contrary;
But soft the wind comes from the sky,
   And whispers tales of Mary.

The night wind whispers in my ear,
   The moon shines in my face;
A burden still of chilling fear
   I find in every place.
The breeze is whispering in the bush,
   And the dews fall from the tree,
All sighing on, and will not hush,
   Some pleasant tales of thee.

The Secret

I loved thee, though I told thee not,
   Right earlily and long,
Thou wert my joy in every spot,
   My theme in every song.

And when I saw a stranger face
   Where beauty held the claim,
I gave it like a secret grace
   The being of thy name.

And all the charms of face or voice
   Which I in others see
Are but the recollected choice
   Of what I felt for thee.

I Hid My Love

I hid my love when young till I
Couldn't bear the buzzing of a fly;
I hid my love to my despite
Till I could not bear to look at light:
I dare not gaze upon her face
But left her memory in each place;
Where'er I saw a wild flower lie
I kissed and bade my love good-bye.

I met her in the greenest dells,
Where dewdrops pearl the wood bluebells;
The lost breeze kissed her bright blue eye,
The bee kissed and went singing by,
A sunbeam found a passage there,
A gold chain round her neck so fair;
As secret as the wild bee's song
She lay there all the summer long.

I hid my love in field and town
Till e'en the breeze would knock me down;
The bees seemed singing ballads o'er,
The fly's bass turned a lion's roar;
And even silence found a tongue,
To haunt me all the summer long;
The riddle nature could not prove
Was nothing else but secret love.

JOHN KEATS
(1795–1821)

'Bright Star, Would I Were Stedfast as Thou Art—'

Bright star, would I were stedfast as thou art—
    Not in lone splendour hung aloft the night
And watching, with eternal lids apart,
    Like nature's patient, sleepless Eremite,

The moving waters at their priestlike task
   Of pure ablution round earth's human shores,
Or gazing on the new soft-fallen mask
   Of snow upon the mountains and the moors—
No—yet still stedfast, still unchangeable,
   Pillow'd upon my fair love's ripening breast,
To feel for ever its soft fall and swell,
   Awake for ever in a sweet unrest,
Still, still to hear her tender-taken breath,
And so live ever—or else swoon to death.

THOMAS HOOD
(1799–1845)

Ruth

She stood breast-high amid the corn,
Clasp'd by the golden light of morn,
Like the sweetheart of the sun,
Who many a glowing kiss had won.

On her cheek an autumn flush,
Deeply ripen'd;—such a blush
In the midst of brown was born,
Like red poppies grown with corn.

Round her eyes her tresses fell,
Which were blackest none could tell,
But long lashes veil'd a light,
That had else been all too bright.

And her hat, with shady brim,
Made her tressy forehead dim;
Thus she stood amid the stooks,
Praising God with sweetest looks:—

Sure, I said, Heav'n did not mean,
Where I reap thou shouldst but glean,
Lay thy sheaf adown and come,
Share my harvest and my home.

WILLIAM BARNES
(1801–1886)

The Wife A-Lost

Since I noo mwore do zee your feäce,
    Up steäirs or down below,
I'll zit me in the lwonesome pleäce,
    Where flat-bough'd beech do grow;
Below the beeches' bough, my love,
    Where you did never come,
An' I don't look to meet ye now,
    As I do look at hwome.

Since you noo mwore be at my zide,
    In walks in zummer het,
I'll goo alwone where mist do ride,
    Drough trees a-drippen wet;
Below the raïn-wet bough, my love,
    Where you did never come,
An' I don't grieve to miss ye now,
    As I do grieve at hwome.

Since now bezide my dinner-bwoard
    Your vaïce do never sound,
I'll eat the bit I can avvword,
    A-yield upon the ground;
Below the darksome bough, my love,
    Where you did never dine,
An' I don't grieve to miss ye now,
    As I at hwome do pine.

Since I do miss your vaïce an' feäce
    In praÿer at eventide,
I'll praÿ wi' woone sad vaïce vor greäce
    To goo where you do bide;
Above the tree an' bough, my love,
    Where you be gone avore,
An' be a-waïten vor me now,
    To come vor evermwore.

RALPH WALDO EMERSON
(1803–1882)

Give All to Love

Give all to love;
Obey thy heart;
Friends, kindred, days,
Estate, good fame,
Plans, credit, and the Muse—
Nothing refuse.

'Tis a brave master;
Let it have scope:
Follow it utterly,
Hope beyond hope:
High and more high
It dives into noon,
With wing unspent,
Untold intent;
But it is a god,
Knows its own path,
And the outlets of the sky.

It was never for the mean;
It requireth courage stout,
Souls above doubt,
Valour unbending:
Such 'twill reward;—
They shall return
More than they were,
And ever ascending.

Leave all for love;
Yet, hear me, yet,
One word more thy heart behoved,
One pulse more of firm endeavour—
Keep thee to-day,
To-morrow, for ever,
Free as an Arab
Of thy beloved.

Cling with life to the maid;
But when the surprise,
First vague shadow of surmise,
Flits across her bosom young,
Of a joy apart from thee,
Free be she, fancy-free;
Nor thou detain her vesture's hem,
Nor the palest rose she flung
From her summer diadem.

Though thou loved her as thyself,
As a self of purer clay;
Though her parting dims the day,
Stealing grace from all alive;
Heartily know,
When half-gods go
The gods arrive.

ELIZABETH BARRETT BROWNING
(1806–1861)

'I Thought Once How Theocritus Had Sung'

I thought once how Theocritus had sung
Of the sweet years, the dear and wished-for years,
Who each one in a gracious hand appears
To bear a gift for mortals, old or young:
And, as I mused it in his antique tongue,
I saw, in gradual vision through my tears,
The sweet, sad years, the melancholy years,
Those of my own life, who by turns had flung
A shadow across me. Straightway I was 'ware,
So weeping, how a mystic Shape did move
Behind me, and drew me backward by the hair:
And a voice said in mastery, while I strove,—
'Guess now who holds thee?'—'Death,' I said. But, there,
The silver answer rang,—'Not Death, but Love.'

'How Do I Love Thee? Let Me Count the Ways'

How do I love thee? Let me count the ways.
I love thee to the depth and breadth and height
My soul can reach, when feeling out of sight
For the ends of Being and ideal Grace.
I love thee to the level of everyday's
Most quiet need, by sun and candle-light.
I love thee freely, as men strive for Right;
I love thee purely, as they turn from Praise.
I love thee with the passion put to use
In my old griefs, and with my childhood's faith.
I love thee with a love I seemed to lose
With my lost saints,—I love thee with the breath,
Smiles, tears, of all my life!—and, if God choose,
I shall but love thee better after death.

EDGAR ALLAN POE
(1809–1849)

To Helen

Helen, thy beauty is to me
  Like those Nicéan barks of yore,
That gently, o'er a perfumed sea,
  The weary, way-worn wanderer bore
  To his own native shore.

On desperate seas long wont to roam,
  Thy hyacinth hair, thy classic face,
Thy Naiad airs have brought me home
  To the glory that was Greece,
  And the grandeur that was Rome.

Lo! in yon brilliant window-niche
  How statue-like I see thee stand,
The agate lamp within thy hand!
  Ah, Psyche, from the regions which
  Are Holy-Land!

To One in Paradise

Thou wast that all to me, love,
    For which my soul did pine—
A green isle in the sea, love,
    A fountain and a shrine,
All wreathed with fairy fruits and flowers
    And all the flowers were mine.

Ah, dream too bright to last!
    Ah, starry Hope! that didst arise
But to be overcast!
    A voice from out the Future cries,
"On! on!"—but o'er the Past
    (Dim gulf!) my spirit hovering lies
Mute, motionless, aghast!

For, alas! alas! with me
    The light of Life is o'er!
    "No more—no more—no more—"
(Such language holds the solemn sea
    To the sands upon the shore)
Shall bloom the thunder-blasted tree,
    Or the stricken eagle soar!

And all my days are trances,
    And all my nightly dreams
Are where thy dark eye glances,
    And where thy footstep gleams—
In what ethereal dances,
    By what eternal streams.

Annabel Lee

It was many and many a year ago,
    In a kingdom by the sea,
That a maiden there lived whom you may know
    By the name of ANNABEL LEE;
And this maiden she lived with no other thought
    Than to love and be loved by me.

I was a child and *she* was a child,
    In this kingdom by the sea:
But we loved with a love that was more than love—
    I and my ANNABEL LEE;
With a love that the winged seraphs of heaven
    Coveted her and me.

And this was the reason that, long ago,
    In this kingdom by the sea,
A wind blew out of a cloud, chilling
    My beautiful ANNABEL LEE;
So that her high-born kinsman came
    And bore her away from me,
To shut her up in a sepulchre
    In this kingdom by the sea.

The angels, not half so happy in heaven,
    Went envying her and me—
Yes!—that was the reason (as all men know,
    In this kingdom by the sea)
That the wind came out of the cloud by night,
    Chilling and killing my ANNABEL LEE.

But our love it was stronger by far than the love
    Of those who were older than we—
    Of many far wiser than we—
And neither the angels in heaven above,
    Nor the demons down under the sea,
Can ever dissever my soul from the soul
    Of the beautiful ANNABEL LEE,

For the moon never beams, without bringing me dreams
    Of the beautiful ANNABEL LEE;

And the stars never rise, but I feel the bright eyes
    Of the beautiful ANNABEL LEE;
And so, all the night-tide, I lie down by the side
Of my darling—my darling—my life and my bride,
    In the sepulchre there by the sea,
    In her tomb by the sounding sea.

ALFRED, LORD TENNYSON
(1809–1892)

'Now Sleeps the Crimson Petal, Now the White'

Now sleeps the crimson petal, now the white;
Nor waves the cypress in the palace walk;
Nor winks the gold fin in the porphyry font:
The firefly wakens: waken thou with me.

Now droops the milk-white peacock like a ghost,
And like a ghost she glimmers on to me.

Now lies the Earth all Danaë to the stars,
And all thy heart lies open unto me.

Now slides the silent meteor on, and leaves
A shining furrow, as thy thoughts in me.

Now folds the lily all her sweetness up,
And slips into the bosom of the lake:
So fold thyself, my dearest, thou, and slip
Into my bosom and be lost in me.

'Come Not, When I Am Dead'

Come not, when I am dead,
    To drop thy foolish tears upon my grave,
To trample round my fallen head,
    And vex the unhappy dust thou wouldst not save.

There let the wind sweep and the plover cry;
    But thou, go by.

Child, if it were thine error or thy crime
    I care no longer, being all unblest:
Wed whom thou wilt, but I am sick of Time,
    And I desire to rest.
Pass on, weak heart, and leave me where I lie;
    Go by, go by.

ROBERT BROWNING

(1812–1889)

The Last Ride Together

I said—Then, dearest, since 'tis so,
Since now at length my fate I know,
Since nothing all my love avails,
Since all, my life seemed meant for, fails,
    Since this was written and needs must be—
My whole heart rises up to bless
Your name in pride and thankfulness!
Take back the hope you gave, I claim
Only a memory of the same,
—And this beside, if you will not blame,
    Your leave for one more last ride with me.

My mistress bent that brow of hers;
Those deep dark eyes where pride demurs
When pity would be softening through,
Fixed me a breathing-while or two
    With life or death in the balance: right!
The blood replenished me again;
My last thought was at least not vain:
I and my mistress, side by side
Shall be together, breathe and ride,
So, one day more am I deified.
    Who knows but the world may end tonight?

Hush! if you saw some western cloud
All billowy-bosomed, over-bowed
By many benedictions—sun's
And moon's and evening-star's at once—
   And so, you, looking and loving best,
Conscious grew, your passion drew
Cloud, sunset, moonrise, star-shine too,
Down on you, near and yet more near,
Till flesh must fade for heaven was here!—
Thus leant she and lingered—joy and fear!
   Thus lay she a moment on my breast.

Then we began to ride. My soul
Smoothed itself out, a long-cramped scroll
Freshening and fluttering in the wind.
Past hopes already lay behind.
   What need to strive with a life awry?
Had I said that, had I done this,
So might I gain, so might I miss.
Might she have loved me? just as well
She might have hated, who can tell!
Where had I been now if the worst befell?
   And here we are riding, she and I.

Fail I alone, in words and deeds?
Why, all men strive and who succeeds?
We rode; it seemed my spirit flew,
Saw other regions, cities new,
   As the world rushed by on either side.
I thought,—All labour, yet no less
Bear up beneath their unsuccess.
Look at the end of work, contrast
The petty done, the undone vast,
This present of theirs with the hopeful past!
   I hoped she would love me; here we ride.

What hand and brain went ever paired?
What heart alike conceived and dared?
What act proved all its thought had been?
What will but felt the fleshly screen?
   We ride and I see her bosom heave.
There's many a crown for who can reach.

Ten lines, a statesman's life in each!
The flag stuck on a heap of bones,
A soldier's doing! what atones?
They scratch his name on the Abbey-stones.
    My riding is better, by their leave.

What does it all mean, poet? Well,
Your brains beat into rhythm, you tell
What we felt only; you expressed
You hold things beautiful the best,
    And pace them in rhyme so, side by side.
'Tis something, nay 'tis much: but then,
Have you yourself what's best for men?
Are you—poor, sick, old ere your time—
Nearer one whit your own sublime
Than we who never have turned a rhyme?
    Sing, riding's a joy! For me, I ride.

And you, great sculptor—so, you gave
A score of years to Art, her slave,
And that's your Venus, whence we turn
To yonder girl that fords the burn!
    You acquiesce, and shall I repine?
What, man of music, you grown grey
With notes and nothing else to say,
Is this your sole praise from a friend,
'Greatly his opera's strains intend,
'But in music we know how fashions end!'
    I gave my youth; but we ride, in fine.

Who knows what's fit for us? Had fate
Proposed bliss here should sublimate
My being—had I signed the bond—
Still one must lead some life beyond,
    Have a bliss to die with, dim-descried.
This foot once planted on the goal,
This glory-garland round my soul,
Could I descry such? Try and test!
I sink back shuddering from the quest.
Earth being so good, would heaven seem best?
    Now, heaven and she are beyond this ride.

And yet—she has not spoke so long!
What if heaven be that, fair and strong
At life's best, with our eyes upturned
Whither life's flower is first discerned,
    We, fixed so, ever should so abide?
What if we still ride on, we two
With life for ever old yet new,
Changed not in kind but in degree
The instant made eternity,—
And heaven just prove that I and she
    Ride, ride together, for ever ride?

Meeting at Night

The gray sea and the long black land;
And the yellow half-moon large and low;
And the startled little waves that leap
In fiery ringlets from their sleep,
As I gain the cove with pushing prow,
And quench its speed i' the slushy sand.

Then a mile of warm sea-scented beach;
Three fields to cross till a farm appears;
A tap at the pane, the quick sharp scratch
And blue spurt of a lighted match,
And a voice less loud, thro' its joys and fears,
Than the two hearts beating each to each!

Bad Dreams

Last night I saw you in my sleep:
    And how your charm of face was changed!
I asked, 'Some love, some faith you keep?'
    You answered, 'Faith gone, love estranged.'

Whereat I woke—a twofold bliss:
  Waking was one, but next there came
This other: 'Though I felt, for this,
  My heart break, I loved on the same.'

Love

So, the year's done with!
  (*Love me for ever!*)
All March begun with,
  April's endeavour;
May-wreaths that bound me
  June needs must sever;
Now snows fall round me,
  Quenching June's fever—
  (*Love me for ever!*)

EMILY BRONTË
(1818–1848)

Remembrance

Cold in the earth—and the deep snow piled above thee,
  Far, far removed, cold in the dreary grave!
Have I forgot, my only Love, to love thee,
  Severed at last by Time's all-severing wave?

Now, when alone, do my thoughts no longer hover
  Over the mountains, on that northern shore,
Resting their wings where heath and fern-leaves cover
  Thy noble heart for ever, ever more?

Cold in the earth—and fifteen wild Decembers
  From those brown hills, have melted into spring:

Faithful, indeed, is the spirit that remembers
    After such years of change and suffering!

Sweet Love of youth, forgive, if I forget thee,
    While the world's tide is bearing me along;
Other desires and other hopes beset me,
    Hopes which obscure, but cannot do thee wrong!

No later light has lightened up my heaven,
    No second morn has ever shone for me;
All my life's bliss from thy dear life was given,
    All my life's bliss is in the grave with thee.

But when the days of golden dreams had perished,
    And even Despair was powerless to destroy,
Then did I learn how existence could be cherished,
    Strengthened, and fed, without the aid of joy.

Then did I check the tears of useless passion—
    Weaned my young soul from yearning after thine;
Sternly denied its burning wish to hasten
    Down to that tomb already more than mine.

And, even yet, I dare not let it languish,
    Dare not indulge in memory's rapturous pain;
Once drinking deep of that divinest anguish,
    How could I seek the empty world again?

'If Grief for Grief Can Touch Thee'

If grief for grief can touch thee,
If answering woe for woe,
If any ruth can melt thee,
Come to me now!

I cannot be more lonely,
More drear I cannot be!
My worn heart throbs so wildly
'Twill break for thee.

And when the world despises,
When heaven repels my prayer,

Will not mine angel comfort?
Mine idol hear?

Yes, by the tears I've poured thee,
By all my hours of pain,
O I shall surely win thee,
Beloved, again!

WALT WHITMAN
(1819–1892)

Once I Pass'd through a Populous City

Once I pass'd through a populous city imprinting my brain for
    future use with its shows, architecture, customs, traditions,
Yet now of all that city I remember only a woman I casually met
    there who detain'd me for love of me,
Day by day and night by night we were together—all else has long
    been forgotten by me,
I remember I say only that woman who passionately clung to me,
Again we wander, we love, we separate again,
Again she holds me by the hand, I must not go,
I see her close beside me with silent lips sad and tremulous.

When I Heard at the Close of the Day

When I heard at the close of the day how my name had been
    receiv'd with plaudits in the capitol, still it was not a happy
    night for me that follow'd,
And else when I carous'd, or when my plans were accomplish'd,
    still I was not happy,
But the day when I rose at dawn from the bed of perfect health,
    refresh'd, singing, inhaling the ripe breath of autumn,
When I saw the full moon in the west grow pale and disappear in
    the morning light,

When I wander'd alone over the beach, and undressing bathed, laughing with the cool waters, and saw the sun rise,
And when I thought how my dear friend my lover was on his way coming, O then I was happy,
O then each breath tasted sweeter, and all that day my food nourish'd me more, and the beautiful day pass'd well,
And the next came with equal joy, and with the next at evening came my friend,
And that night while all was still I heard the waters roll slowly continually up the shores,
I heard the hissing rustle of the liquid and sands as directed to me whispering to congratulate me,
For the one I love most lay sleeping by me under the same cover in the cool night,
In the stillness in the autumn moonbeams his face was inclined toward me,
And his arm lay lightly around my breast—and that night I was happy.

Sometimes with One I Love

Sometimes with one I love I fill myself with rage for fear I effuse unreturn'd love,
But now I think there is no unreturn'd love, the pay is certain one way or another,
(I loved a certain person ardently and my love was not return'd,
Yet out of that I have written these songs.)

As if a Phantom Caress'd Me

As if a phantom caress'd me,
I thought I was not alone walking here by the shore;
But the one I thought was with me as now I walk by the shore, the one I loved that caress'd me,
As I lean and look through the glimmering light, that one has utterly disappear'd,
And those appear that are hateful to me and mock me.

From Pent-Up Aching Rivers

From pent-up aching rivers,
From that of myself without which I were nothing,
From what I am determin'd to make illustrous, even if I stand sole
    among men,
From my own voice resonant, singing the phallus,
Singing the song of procreation,
Singing the need of superb children and therein superb grown
    people,
Singing the muscular urge and the blending,
Singing the bedfellow's song, (O resistless yearning!
O for any and each the body correlative attracting!
O for you whoever you are your correlative body! O it, more than
    all else, you delighting!)
From the hungry gnaw that eats me night and day,
From native moments, from bashful pains, singing them,
Seeking something yet unfound though I have diligently sought it
    many a long year,
Singing the true song of the soul fitful at random,
Renascent with grossest Nature or among animals,
Of that, of them and what goes with them my poems informing,
Of the smell of apples and lemons, of the pairing of birds,
Of the wet of woods, of the lapping of waves,
Of the mad pushes of waves upon the land, I them chanting,
The overture lightly sounding, the strain anticipating,
The welcome nearness, the sight of the perfect body,
The swimmer swimming naked in the bath, or motionless on his
    back lying and floating,
The female form approaching, I pensive, love-flesh tremulous
    aching,
The divine list for myself or you or for any one making,
The face, the limbs, the index from head to foot, and what it
    arouses,
The mystic deliria, the madness amorous, the utter abandonment,
(Hark close and still what I now whisper to you,
I love you, O you entirely possess me,
O that you and I escape from the rest and go utterly off, free and
    lawless,

Two hawks in the air, two fishes swimming in the sea not more
    lawless than we;)
The furious storm through me careering, I passionately trembling,
The oath of the inseparableness of two together, of the woman that
    loves me and whom I love more than my life, that oath
    swearing,
(O I willingly stake all for you,
O let me be lost if it must be so!
O you and I! what is it to us what the rest do or think?
What is all else to us? only that we enjoy each other and exhaust
    each other if it must be so;)
From the master, the pilot I yield the vessel to,
The general commanding me, commanding all, from him permis-
    sion taking,
From time the programme hastening, (I have loiter'd too long as it
    is,)
From sex, from the warp and from the woof,
From privacy, from frequent repinings alone,
From plenty of persons near and yet the right person not near,
From the soft sliding of hands over me and thrusting of fingers
    through my hair and beard,
From the long sustain'd kiss upon the mouth or bosom,
From the close pressure that makes me or any man drunk, fainting
    with excess,
From what the divine husband knows, from the work of father-
    hood,
From exultation, victory and relief from the bedfellow's embrace in
    the night,
From the act-poems of eyes, hands, hips and bosoms,
From the cling of the trembling arm,
From the bending curve and the clinch,
From side by side the pliant coverlet off-throwing,
From the one so unwilling to have me leave, and me just as
    unwilling to leave,
(Yet a moment O tender waiter, and I return,)
From the hour of shining stars and dropping dews,
From the night a moment I emerging flitting out,
Celebrate you act divine and you children prepared for,
And you stalwart loins.

MATTHEW ARNOLD
(1822–1888)

Longing

Come to me in my dreams, and then
By day I shall be well again.
For then the night will more than pay
The hopeless longing of the day.

Come, as thou cam'st a thousand times
A messenger from the radiant climes,
And smile on thy new world, and be
As kind to others as to me.

Or, as thou never cam'st in sooth,
Come now, and let me dream it truth.
And part my hair, and kiss my brow,
And say—My love! why sufferest thou?

Come to me in my dreams, and then
By day I shall be well again.
For then the night will more than pay
The hopeless longing of the day.

Absence

In this fair stranger's eyes of grey
Thine eyes, my love, I see.
I shudder: for the passing day
Had borne me far from thee.

This is the curse of life: that not
A nobler calmer train
Of wiser thoughts and feelings blot
Our passions from our brain;

But each day brings its petty dust
Our soon-chok'd souls to fill,
And we forget because we must,
And not because we will.

I struggle towards the light; and ye,
Once-long'd-for storms of love!
If with the light ye cannot be,
I bear that ye remove.

I struggle towards the light; but oh,
While yet the night is chill,
Upon Time's barren, stormy flow,
Stay with me, Marguerite, still!

COVENTRY PATMORE
(1823–1896)

The Revelation

An idle poet, here and there,
    Looks round him; but, for all the rest,
The world, unfathomably fair,
    Is duller than a witling's jest.
Love wakes men, once a lifetime each;
    They lift their heavy lids, and look;
And, lo, what one sweet page can teach
    They read with joy, then shut the book.
And some give thanks, and some blaspheme,
    And most forget; but, either way,
That and the Child's unheeded dream
Is all the light of all their day.

A Farewell

With all my will, but much against my heart,
We two now part.
My Very Dear,
Our solace is, the sad road lies so clear.
It needs no art,
With faint, averted feet
And many a tear,
In our opposed paths to persevere.
Go thou to East, I West.
We will not say
There's any hope, it is so far away
But, O, my Best,
When the one darling of our widowhead,
The nursling Grief,
Is dead,
And no dews blur our eyes
To see the peach-bloom come in evening skies,
Perchance we may,
Where now this night is day,
And even through faith of still averted feet,
Making full circle of our banishment,
Amazed meet;
The bitter journey to the bourne so sweet
Seasoning the termless feast of our content
With tears of recognition never dry.

The Azalea

There, where the sun shines first
Against our room,
She train'd the gold Azalea, whose perfume
She, Spring-like, from her breathing grace dispersed.
Last night the delicate crests of saffron bloom,
For this their dainty likeness watch'd and nurst,

Were just at point to burst.
At dawn I dream'd, O God, that she was dead,
And groan'd aloud upon my wretched bed,
And waked, ah, God, and did not waken her,
But lay, with eyes still closed,
Perfectly bless'd in the delicious sphere
By which I knew so well that she was near,
My heart to speechless thankfulness composed.
Till 'gan to stir
A dizzy somewhat in my troubled head—
It *was* the azalea's breath, and she *was* dead!
The warm night had the lingering buds disclosed,
And I had fall'n asleep with to my breast
A chance-found letter press'd
In which she said,
'So, till to-morrow eve, my Own, adieu!
Parting's well-paid with soon again to meet,
Soon in your arms to feel so small and sweet,
Sweet to myself that am so sweet to you!'

DANTE GABRIEL ROSSETTI
(1828–1882)

Sudden Light

I have been here before,
    But when or how I cannot tell:
I know the grass beyond the door,
    The sweet keen smell,
The sighing sound, the lights around the shore.

You have been mine before,
    How long ago I may not know:
But just when at that swallow's soar
    Your neck turned so,
Some veil did fall—I knew it all of yore.

Has this been thus before?
    And shall not thus time's eddying flight

Still with our lives our love restore
    In death's despite,
And day and night yield one delight once more?

Silent Noon

Your hands lie open in the long fresh grass,—
    The finger-points look through like rosy blooms:
    Your eyes smile peace. The pasture gleams and glooms
'Neath billowing skies that scatter and amass.
All round our nest, far as the eye can pass,
    Are golden kingcup-fields with silver edge
    Where the cow-parsley skirts the hawthorn-hedge.
'Tis visible silence, still as the hour-glass.

Deep in the sun-searched growths the dragon-fly
Hangs like a blue thread loosened from the sky:—
    So this wing'd hour is dropt to us from above.
Oh! clasp we to our hearts, for deathless dower,
This close-companioned inarticulate hour
    When twofold silence was the song of love.

Severed Selves

Two separate divided silences,
    Which, brought together, would find loving voice;
    Two glances which together would rejoice
In love, now lost like stars beyond dark trees;
Two hands apart whose touch alone gives ease;
    Two bosoms which, heart-shrined with mutual flame,
    Would, meeting in one clasp, be made the same;
Two souls, the shores wave mocked of sundering seas:—

Such are we now. Ah! may our hope forecast
    Indeed one hour again, when on this stream
    Of darkened love once more the light shall gleam?—

An hour how slow to come, how quickly past,—
Which blooms and fades, and only leaves at last,
Faint as shed flowers, the attenuated dream.

Without Her

What of her glass without her? The blank grey
There where the pool is blind of the moon's face.
Her dress without her? The tossed empty space
Of cloud-rack whence the moon has passed away.
Her paths without her? Day's appointed sway
Usurped by desolate night. Her pillowed place
Without her? Tears, ah me! for love's good grace,
And cold forgetfulness of night or day.

What of the heart without her? Nay, poor heart,
Of thee what word remains ere speech be still?
A wayfarer by barren ways and chill,
Steep ways and weary, without her thou art,
Where the long cloud, the long wood's counterpart,
Sheds doubled darkness up the labouring hill.

The Orchard-Pit

Piled deep below the screening apple-branch
They lie with bitter apples in their hands:
And some are only ancient bones that blanch,
And some had ships that last year's wind did launch,
And some were yesterday the lords of lands.

In the soft dell, among the apple-trees,
High up above the hidden pit she stands,
And there for ever sings, who gave to these,
That lie below, her magic hour of ease,
And those her apples holden in their hands.

This in my dreams is shown me; and her hair
   Crosses my lips and draws my burning breath;
Her song spreads golden wings upon the air,
Life's eyes are gleaming from her forehead fair,
   And from her breasts the ravishing eyes of Death.

Men say to me that sleep hath many dreams,
   Yet I knew never but this dream alone:
There, from a dried-up channel, once the stream's,
The glen slopes up; even such in sleep it seems
   As to my waking sight the place well known.

My love I call her, and she loves me well:
   But I love her as in the maelstrom's cup
The whirled stone loves the leaf inseparable
That clings to it round all the circling swell,
   And that the same last eddy swallows up.

GEORGE MEREDITH
(1828–1909)

'By This He Knew She Wept with Waking Eyes'

By this he knew she wept with waking eyes:
That, at his hand's light quiver by her head,
The strange low sobs that shook their common bed
Were called into her with a sharp surprise,
And strangled mute, like little gaping snakes,
Dreadfully venomous to him. She lay
Stone-still, and the long darkness flowed away
With muffled pulses. Then, as midnight makes
Her giant heart of Memory and Tears
Drink the pale drug of silence, and so beat
Sleep's heavy measure, they from head to feet
Were moveless, looking through their dead black years
By vain regret scrawled over the blank wall.
Like sculptured effigies they might be seen
Upon their marriage-tomb, the sword between;
Each wishing for the sword that severs all.

'In Our Old Shipwrecked Days There Was an Hour'

In our old shipwrecked days there was an hour,
When in the firelight steadily aglow,
Joined slackly, we beheld the red chasm grow
Among the clicking coals. Our library-bower
That eve was left to us: and hushed we sat
As lovers to whom Time is whispering.
From sudden-opened doors we heard them sing:
The nodding elders mixed good wine with chat.
Well knew we that Life's greatest treasure lay
With us, and of it was our talk. "Ah, yes!
Love dies!" I said: I never thought it less.
She yearned to me that sentence to unsay.
Then when the fire domed blackening, I found
Her cheek was salt against my kiss, and swift
Up the sharp scale of sobs her breast did lift:—
Now am I haunted by that taste! that sound!

EMILY DICKINSON
(1830–1886)

'We Outgrow Love Like Other Things'

We outgrow love like other things
   And put it in the drawer,
Till it an antique fashion shows
   Like costumes grandsires wore.

'My Life Closed Twice before Its Close'

My life closed twice before its close;
   It yet remains to see
If Immortality unveil
   A third event to me,

So huge, so hopeless to conceive,
    As these that twice befell.
Parting is all we know of heaven,
    And all we need of hell.

CHRISTINA ROSSETTI
(1830–1909)

A Birthday

My heart is like a singing bird
    Whose nest is in a water'd shoot;
My heart is like an apple-tree
    Whose boughs are bent with thick-set fruit;
My heart is like a rainbow shell
    That paddles in a halcyon sea;
My heart is gladder than all these,
    Because my love is come to me.

Raise me a daïs of silk and down;
    Hang it with vair and purple dyes;
Carve it in doves and pomegranates,
    And peacocks with a hundred eyes;
Work it in gold and silver grapes,
    In leaves and silver fleurs-de-lys;
Because the birthday of my life
    Is come, my love is come to me.

Echo

Come to me in the silence of the night;
    Come in the speaking silence of a dream;
Come with soft rounded cheeks and eyes as bright
    As sunlight on a stream;

Come back in tears,
O memory, hope, love of finished years.

O dream how sweet, too sweet, too bitter sweet,
  Whose wakening should have been in Paradise,
Where souls brimfull of love abide and meet;
  Where thirsting longing eyes
    Watch the slow door
That opening, letting in, lets out no more.

Yet come to me in dreams, that I may live
  My very life again though cold in death:
Come back to me in dreams, that I may give
  Pulse for pulse, breath for breath:
    Speak low, lean low,
As long ago, my love, how long ago.

May

I cannot tell you how it was;
But this I know: it came to pass—
Upon a bright and breezy day
When May was young, ah pleasant May!
As yet the poppies were not born
Between the blades of tender corn;
The last eggs had not hatched as yet,
Nor any bird forgone its mate.

I cannot tell you what it was;
But this I know: it did but pass.
It passed away with sunny May,
With all sweet things it passed away,
And left me old, and cold, and grey.

The First Day

I wish I could remember the first day,
First hour, first moment of your meeting me;
If bright or dim the season, it might be
Summer or winter for aught I can say.
So unrecorded did it slip away,
So blind was I to see and to foresee,
So dull to mark the budding of my tree
That would not blossom yet for many a May.
If only I could recollect it! Such
A day of days! I let it come and go
As traceless as a thaw of bygone snow.
It seemed to mean so little, meant so much!
If only now I could recall that touch,
First touch of hand in hand!—Did one but know!

WILLIAM MORRIS
(1834–1896)

Love Is Enough

Love is enough: though the World be a-waning,
And the woods have no voice but the voice of complaining,
   Though the sky be too dark for dim eyes to discover
The gold-cups and daisies fair blooming thereunder,
Though the hills be held shadows, and the sea a dark wonder
   And this day draw a veil over all deeds pass'd over,
Yet their hands shall not tremble, their feet shall not falter;
The void shall not weary, the fear shall not alter
   These lips and these eyes of the loved and the lover.

ALGERNON CHARLES SWINBURNE
(1837–1909)

Love and Sleep

Lying asleep between the strokes of night
   I saw my love lean over my sad bed,
   Pale as the duskiest lily's leaf or head,
Smooth-skinned and dark, with bare throat made to bite,
Too wan for blushing and too warm for white,
   But perfect-coloured without white or red.
   And her lips opened amorously, and said—
I wist not what, saving one word—Delight.

And all her face was honey to my mouth,
   And all her body pasture to mine eyes;
     The long lithe arms and hotter hands than fire,
The quivering flanks, hair smelling of the south,
   The bright light feet, the splendid supple thighs
     And glittering eyelids of my soul's desire.

WILFRID BLUNT
(1840–1922)

St. Valentine's Day

Today, all day, I rode upon the Down,
With hounds and horsemen, a brave company.
On this side in its glory lay the sea,
On that the Sussex Weald, a sea of brown.
The wind was light, and brightly the sun shone,
And still we galloped on from gorse to gorse.
And once, when checked, a thrush sang, and my horse
Pricked his quick ears as to a sound unknown.
I knew the spring was come. I knew it even
Better than all by this, that through my chase

In bush and stone and hill and sea and heaven
I seemed to see and follow still your face.
Your face my quarry was. For it I rode,
My horse a thing of wings, myself a god.

THOMAS HARDY
(1840–1928)

A Broken Appointment

You did not come,
And marching Time drew on, and wore me numb.
Yet less for loss of your dear presence there
Than that I thus found lacking in your make
That high compassion which can overbear
Reluctance for pure lovingkindness' sake
Grieved I, when, as the hope-hour stroked its sum,
You did not come.

You love not me,
And love alone can lend you loyalty;
—I know and knew it. But, unto the store
Of human deeds divine in all but name,
Was it not worth a little hour or more
To add yet this: Once you, a woman, came
To soothe a time-torn man; even though it be
You love not me?

In a Cathedral City

These people have not heard your name;
No loungers in this placid place
Have helped to bruit your beauty's fame.

The grey Cathedral, towards whose face
Bend eyes untold, has met not yours;
Your shade has never swept its base,

Your form has never darked its doors,
Nor have your faultless feet once thrown
A pensive pit-pat on its floors.

Along the street to maids well known
Blithe lovers hum their tender airs,
But in your praise voice not a tone. . . .

—Since nought bespeaks you here, or bears,
As I, your imprint through and through,
Here might I rest, till my heart shares
The spot's unconsciousness of you!

A Thunderstorm in Town

(A Reminiscence: 1893)

She wore a new 'terra-cotta' dress,
And we stayed, because of the pelting storm,
Within the hansom's dry recess,
Though the horse had stopped; yea, motionless
    We sat on, snug and warm.

Then the downpour ceased, to my sharp sad pain,
And the glass that had screened our forms before
Flew up, and out she sprang to her door:
I should have kissed her if the rain
    Had lasted a minute more.

ALICE MEYNELL

(1847–1922)

Renouncement

I must not think of thee; and, tired yet strong,
I shun the love that lurks in all delight—
    The love of thee—and in the blue heaven's height,
And in the dearest passage of a song.

Oh, just beyond the sweetest thoughts that throng
   This breast, the thought of thee waits hidden yet bright;
But it must never, never come in sight;
I must stop short of thee the whole day long.
But when sleep comes to close each difficult day,
   When night gives pause to the long watch I keep,
And all my bonds I needs must loose apart,
Must doff my will as raiment laid away,—
   With the first dream that comes with the first sleep
I run, I run, I am gather'd to thy heart.

A. E. HOUSMAN
(1859–1936)

'Oh, When I Was in Love with You'

Oh, when I was in love with you,
   Then I was clean and brave,
And miles around the wonder grew
   How well did I behave.

And now the fancy passes by,
   And nothing will remain,
And miles around they'll say that I
   Am quite myself again.

'Along the Field as We Came By'

Along the field as we came by
A year ago, my love and I,
The aspen over stile and stone
Was talking to itself alone.
'Oh who are these that kiss and pass?
A country lover and his lass;
Two lovers looking to be wed;

And time shall put them both to bed,
But she shall lie with earth above,
And he beside another love.'

  And sure enough beneath the tree
There walks another love with me,
And overhead the aspen heaves
Its rainy-sounding silver leaves;
And I spell nothing in their stir,
But now perhaps they speak to her,
And plain for her to understand
They talk about a time at hand
When I shall sleep with clover clad,
And she beside another lad.

'White in the Moon the Long Road Lies'

White in the moon the long road lies,
  The moon stands blank above;
White in the moon the long road lies
  That leads me from my love.

Still hangs the hedge without a gust,
  Still, still the shadows stay:
My feet upon the moonlit dust
  Pursue the ceaseless way.

The world is round, so travellers tell,
  And straight though reach the track,
Trudge on, trudge on, 'twill all be well,
  The way will guide one back.

But ere the circle homeward hies
  Far, far must it remove:
White in the moon the long road lies
  That leads me from my love.

W. B. YEATS
(1864–1939)

Down by the Salley Gardens

Down by the salley gardens my love and I did meet;
She passed the salley gardens with little snow-white feet.
She bid me take love easy, as the leaves grow on the tree;
But I, being young and foolish, with her would not agree.

In a field by the river my love and I did stand,
And on my leaning shoulder she laid her snow-white hand.
She bid me take life easy, as the grass grows on the weirs;
But I was young and foolish, and now am full of tears.

Brown Penny

I whispered, 'I am too young,'
And then, 'I am old enough';
Wherefore I threw a penny
To find out if I might love.
'Go and love, go and love, young man,
If the lady be young and fair.'
Ah, penny, brown penny, brown penny,
I am looped in the loops of her hair.

O love is the crooked thing,
There is nobody wise enough
To find out all that is in it,
For he would be thinking of love
Till the stars had run away
And the shadows eaten the moon.
Ah, penny, brown penny, brown penny,
One cannot begin it too soon.

A Drinking Song

Wine comes in at the mouth
And love comes in at the eye;
That's all we know for truth
Before we grow old and die.
I lift the glass to my mouth,
I look at you, and I sigh.

Never Give All the Heart

Never give all the heart, for love
Will hardly seem worth thinking of
To passionate women if it seem
Certain, and they never dream
That it fades out from kiss to kiss;
For everything that's lovely is
But a brief, dreamy, kind delight.
O never give the heart outright,
For they, for all smooth lips can say,
Have given their hearts up to the play.
And who could play it well enough
If deaf and dumb and blind with love?
He that made this knows all the cost,
For he gave all his heart and lost.

When You Are Old

When you are old and grey and full of sleep,
And nodding by the fire, take down this book,
And slowly read, and dream of the soft look
Your eyes had once, and of their shadows deep;

How many loved your moments of glad grace,
And loved your beauty with love false or true,

But one man loved the pilgrim soul in you,
And loved the sorrows of your changing face;

And bending down beside the glowing bars,
Murmur, a little sadly, how Love fled
And paced upon the mountains overhead
And hid his face amid a crowd of stars.

ARTHUR SYMONS
(1865–1945)

White Heliotrope

The feverish room and that white bed,
The tumbled skirts upon a chair,
The novel flung half-open where
Hat, hair-pins, puffs, and paints, are spread;

The mirror that has sucked your face
Into its secret deep of deeps,
And there mysteriously keeps
Forgotten memories of grace;

And you, half dressed and half awake,
Your slant eyes strangely watching me,
And I, who watch you drowsily,
With eyes that, having slept not, ache;

This (need one dread? nay, dare one hope?)
Will rise, a ghost of memory, if
Ever again my handkerchief
Is scented with White Heliotrope.

ERNEST DOWSON
(1867–1900)

Non sum qualis eram bonae sub regno Cynarae[1]

Last night, ah, yesternight, betwixt her lips and mine
There fell thy shadow, Cynara! thy breath was shed
Upon my soul between the kisses and the wine;
And I was desolate and sick of an old passion,
    Yea, I was desolate and bowed my head:
I have been faithful to thee, Cynara! in my fashion.

All night upon mine heart I felt her warm heart beat,
Night-long within mine arms in love and sleep she lay;
Surely the kisses of her bought red mouth were sweet;
But I was desolate and sick of an old passion,
    When I awoke and found the dawn was gray:
I have been faithful to thee, Cynara! in my fashion.

I have forgot much, Cynara! gone with the wind,
Flung roses, roses riotously with the throng,
Dancing, to put thy pale, lost lilies out of mind;
But I was desolate and sick of an old passion,
    Yea, all the time, because the dance was long:
I have been faithful to thee, Cynara! in my fashion.

I cried for madder music and for stronger wine,
But when the feast is finished and the lamps expire,
Then falls thy shadow, Cynara! the night is thine;
And I am desolate and sick of an old passion,
    Yea hungry for the lips of my desire:
I have been faithful to thee, Cynara! in my fashion.

---

[1] "I Am Not as I Was in the Reign of Kind Cynara." The reference is to a woman in Horace's *Odes* (Book IV, Ode I).

EDWIN ARLINGTON ROBINSON
(1869–1935)

Eros Turannos

She fears him, and will always ask
   What fated her to choose him;
She meets in his engaging mask
   All reasons to refuse him;
But what she meets and what she fears
Are less than are the downward years,
Drawn slowly to the foamless weirs
   Of age, were she to lose him.

Between a blurred sagacity
   That once had power to sound him,
And Love, that will not let him be
   The Judas that she found him,
Her pride assuages her almost,
As if it were alone the cost.
He sees that he will not be lost,
   And waits and looks around him.

A sense of ocean and old trees
   Envelopes and allures him;
Tradition, touching all he sees,
   Beguiles and reassures him;
And all her doubts of what he says
Are dimmed with what she knows of days—
Till even prejudice delays
   And fades, and she secures him.

The falling leaf inaugurates
   The reign of her confusion;
The pounding wave reverberates
   The dirge of her illusion;
And home, where passion lived and died,
Becomes a place where she can hide,
While all the town and harbor side
   Vibrate with her seclusion.

We tell you, tapping on our brows,
   The story as it should be,
As if the story of a house
   Were told, or ever could be;
We'll have no kindly veil between
Her visions and those we have seen,
As if we guessed what hers have been,
   Or what they are or would be.

Meanwhile we do no harm; for they
   That with a god have striven,
Not hearing much of what we say,
   Take what the god has given;
Though like waves breaking it may be,
Or like a changed familiar tree,
Or like a stairway to the sea
   Where down the blind are driven.

HILAIRE BELLOC
(1870–1953)

Juliet

How did the party go in Portman Square?
I cannot tell you; Juliet was not there.

And how did Lady Gaster's party go?
Juliet was next me and I do not know.

ROBERT FROST
(1874–1963)

Meeting and Passing

As I went down the hill along the wall
There was a gate I had leaned at for the view
And had just turned from when I first saw you
As you came up the hill. We met. But all

We did that day was mingle great and small
Footprints in summer dust as if we drew
The figure of our being less than two
But more than one as yet. Your parasol

Pointed the decimal off with one deep thrust.
And all the time we talked you seemed to see
Something down there to smile at in the dust.
(Oh, it was without prejudice to me!)
Afterward I went past what you had passed
Before we met and you what I had passed.

D. H. LAWRENCE
(1885–1930)

Gloire de Dijon

When she rises in the morning
I linger to watch her;
She spreads the bath-cloth underneath the window
And the sunbeams catch her
Glistening white on the shoulders,
While down her sides the mellow
Golden shadow glows as
She stoops to the sponge, and her swung breasts
Sway like full-blown yellow
Gloire de Dijon roses.

She drips herself with water, and her shoulders
Glisten as silver, they crumple up
Like wet and falling roses, and I listen
For the sluicing of their rain-dishevelled petals.
In the window full of sunlight
Concentrates her golden shadow
Fold on fold, until it glows as
Mellow as the glory roses.

EZRA POUND
(1885–1972)

The River-Merchant's Wife: A Letter

Translated from the Chinese of Li Po [Rihaku]

While my hair was still cut straight across my forehead
I played about the front gate, pulling flowers.
You came by on bamboo stilts, playing horse,
You walked about my seat, playing with blue plums.
And we went on living in the village of Chokan:
Two small people, without dislike or suspicion.

At fourteen I married My Lord you.
I never laughed, being bashful.
Lowering my head, I looked at the wall.
Called to, a thousand times, I never looked back.

At fifteen I stopped scowling,
I desired my dust to be mingled with yours
Forever and forever and forever.
Why should I climb the look out?

At sixteen you departed,
You went into far Ku-to-yen, by the river of swirling eddies,
And you have been gone five months.
The monkeys make sorrowful noise overhead.
You dragged your feet when you went out.
By the gate now, the moss is grown, the different mosses,
Too deep to clear them away!
The leaves fall early this autumn, in wind.
The paired butterflies are already yellow with August
Over the grass in the West garden;
They hurt me. I grow older.
If you are coming down through the narrows of the river Kiang,
Please let me know beforehand,
And I will come out to meet you
            As far as Cho-fu-sa.

EDWARD THOMAS
(1887–1917)

Like the Touch of Rain

Like the touch of rain she was
On a man's flesh and hair and eyes
When the joy of walking thus
Has taken him by surprise:

With the love of the storm he burns,
He sings, he laughs, well I know how,
But forgets when he returns
As I shall not forget her "Go now."

Those two words shut a door
Between me and the blessed rain
That was never shut before
And will not open again.

JOHN CROWE RANSOM
(1888–1974)

Piazza Piece

—I am a gentleman in a dustcoat trying
To make you hear. Your ears are soft and small
And listen to an old man not at all,
They want the young men's whispering and sighing.
But see the roses on your trellis dying
And hear the spectral singing of the moon;
For I must have my lovely lady soon,
I am a gentleman in a dustcoat trying.

—I am a lady young in beauty waiting
Until my truelove comes, and then we kiss.
But what grey man among the vines is this

Whose words are dry and faint as in a dream?
Back from my trellis, Sir, before I scream!
I am a lady young in beauty waiting.

EDNA ST. VINCENT MILLAY
(1892–1950)

'I, Being Born a Woman and Distressed'

I, being born a woman and distressed
By all the needs and notions of my kind,
Am urged by your propinquity to find
Your person fair, and feel a certain zest
To bear your body's weight upon my breast:
So subtly is the fume of life designed,
To clarify the pulse and cloud the mind,
And leave me once again undone, possessed.
Think not for this, however, the poor treason
Of my stout blood against my staggering brain,
I shall remember you with love, or season
My scorn with pity,—let me make it plain:
I find this frenzy insufficient reason
For conversation when we meet again.

HART CRANE
(1899–1932)

Carrier Letter

My hands have not touched water since your hands,—
No;—nor my lips freed laughter since 'farewell'.
And with the day, distance again expands
Between us, voiceless as an uncoiled shell.

Yet,—much follows, much endures . . . Trust birds alone:
A dove's wings clung about my heart last night
With surging gentleness; and the blue stone
Set in the tryst-ring has but worn more bright.

Alphabetical List of Titles and First Lines

(Where the title is the same as the first line of
a poem, only the former is given.)